SCOT

GREEN

The *Alternative* Guide
to Vegetarian & Vegan Hideaways in Scotland

incorporating the Vegetarian Guide to the Scottish Highlands and Islands

Jackie Redding

DOM + MANDY THEAKER
4 EAST VIEW
ROWLANDS GILL
TYNE & WEAR NE39 2LQ

FINDHORN
Press

Each year tens of millions of wild animals are either trapped in the wild or reared in fur factory farms and killed simply for the fur on their backs to make fur coats.

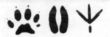

It is quite unnecessary to export live farm animals from this country but we do - condemning them to nightmare journeys and horrific deaths.

There is one organisation that campaigns to end both of these terrible abuses and that has already succeeded in making significant progress. That organisation is: Respect for Animals.

But much more needs to be done to end the suffering and funds are urgently needed for the work to continue. Please find out more and please support Respect for Animals with a donation - today.

respect
RESPECT FOR ANIMALS

P.O. Box 500, Nottingham NG1 3AS
Telephone: 0115 952 5440

CONTENTS

Introduction	5
Scotland	7
Localisms	8
The Scottish Midge	9
The Weather	11
Key to Facilities	13
Travelling North	14
Southern Scotland	15
Central Scotland	19
South East Highlands	27
South West Highlands	31
Aberdeen & Grampian	37
The Highlands & Skye	43
The Map	49
Western Isles, Orkney & Shetland	73
Island Hopping	79
Veggie Retailers	80
Questionaire	94
A-Z Listing	96

THANK YOU!

- *To Janey Clarke and Lori Forsyth who brought the guide this far and trusted me to take it further*
- *To Findhorn Press as always, for their faith and patience*
- *To the advertisers for their trust and help with the editorial*
- *To Celia and Fiona who helped out when there was too much work at the end of the hours*
- *and finally to Tony – I'm sure he must have done something*

4

only after the last tree has been cut down

only after the last river has been poisoned

only after the last fish has been caught

only then will you find that money can not be eaten

THE WISE ONES?

Homo sapiens – the wise one?

on earth as it is in heaven

thy will has been done

You've poisoned the rivers

the fish are diseased

your sisters are starving

but the investors are pleased

Your children have asthma

the cows have gone mad

the forests are burning

but McJunkfood are glad

When will you learn

you *can't* eat your cash

you *can't* breathe investments

nor drink all your trash

Tony Weston © 1996

Welcome to the 8th edition of the 'Vegetarian Guide to the Highlands and Islands' and the very 1st edition of 'Scotland the Green'.

The Veggie guide has been around for a while now and things have changed for both Vegetarianism and for Scotland, so I thought it was time for a change and a face lift (the guide that is, not me!)

The main difference is that this guide covers the whole of Scotland and it also includes health food shops and attractions as well as the usual array of B&Bs, guest houses, restaurants and hotels.

I do hope you like it; if you do, please let me know, and if you don't, also let me know and I'll blame my partner, Tony!

Seriously, I have tried to get it right but the information is taken on trust, I was not able to visit everywhere (I'm working on it) and sometimes things go wrong.

As guesthouse owners ourselves, we would advise, if you have a problem, to bring it to the attention of the establishment immediately – most things can be sorted out. All the places listed are committed to doing good Veggie food, but there seems to be so many categories of Vegetarian these days that it is always best to explain to the proprietor what you do and don't eat to prevent any mishaps.

The information held in this guide is true to the best of my knowledge, however, mistakes and changes do occur so it is always best to check details before you book, particularly in relation to prices quoted.

With this book, I have tried to impart a little of my knowledge of living here. As I live in the Highlands, there may be a little bias in that direction, hopefully no offence will be taken.

The next edition of this guide will be published in early 1999. Please feel free to write to me (using the 'freepost' address at the end) to let me know which places you liked (and which you didn't like).Also, if you find somewhere that isn't included but in your opinion should be – please let me know.

Have a happy holiday!

Jackie
x

*un*caged

END VIVISECTION

contact:
14 ridgeway road sheffield s12 2ss

Whether this is your first visit to Scotland or the most recent of many – I'm sure you will find something different. Scotland is whatever you want it to be, from the beautiful cities of Edinburgh and Glasgow with shops, theatres, clubs and loads of 'happening' to the heritage of the borders and the wilderness of the Highlands.

For some people Scotland means history and legend, from Robert the Bruce to Braveheart and from the Loch Ness Monster to the Haggis. For others, it is the splendour of the scenery, the diversity of the entertainment or the incredible selection of wildlife. Whatever your dreams, they are here just waiting to be discovered.

If this is your first visit to Scotland there is one thing you need to be aware of, Scotland is HUGE. Birmingham is closer to Glasgow than Ullapool is, and the Highlands alone are roughly the size of Belgium! However, the roads are good and it won't be as bad as you may fear. It takes about 6 hours to drive from London to Glasgow and another 5 before you'd fall off the end. So with just one stop-over in the Lakes (see page 14) it will be fine. Better still, you could be environmentally friendly and use public transport - see useful numbers below.

When compiling this book, I tried to fit in with the new tourist board areas, but this is easier said than done. With boundaries changing daily, big opposition from the locals not to remain where they were put and my appalling geography, at one point I was going to call this book 'Where the bloody well are we?'. (Which in actual fact some people preferred to 'Scotland the Green' but that's another story.)

Anyway I've tried to be logical (guys, beware – this is women's logic) in my movements from one area to another. Unfortunately, what was logical to me is not necessarily congruent with to the Scottish Tourist Board's logic, and is probably not at all logical to you – in which case I am sorry, I really tried.

If the Islands are as big a mystery to you as they were to me when I first arrived in Scotland, you will be glad of the Island listing on page 79 which explains where they are and how to get to them.

Useful Numbers			
Rail:	*0345 484950*	*Caledonian MacBrayne*	*01475 650150*
British Airways	*0345 222111*	*P & O Ferries*	*01224 572615*
National Express	*0990 808080*		

LOCALISMS

The Language

Scots speak a kind of English in as much as Brummies, Geordies or Cornish people do – I've lived here for two years now and I still have problems. So here are the main differences that I've picked up. (As I live in the Highlands some of these may not be relevant to other parts of Scotland – but you'll get the gist.)

'Aye' means 'yes', i.e. Och Aye – oh yes – this is something that you will find the incomers say more than the locals these days.

'How?' can sometimes mean 'Why?' as in "can I have some cake" "no!", "how not?". 'Will' appears to mean 'shall' – "will I put my coat on". Yes, this is all true, or maybe my daughter is winding me up.

"Where do you stay?" means "where do you live?", not "where are you staying whilst on holidays" – very confusing!

'Wee' means 'little' and 'dram' means 'whisky'. "Wee dram" appears to mean large whisky!

And finally a couple of misapprehensions: some Scots speak Gaelic pronounced Ga-lic and not Gay-lic which is Irish (although some of the words are the same).

The natives of Scotland are Scots or Scottish, nothing in Scotland is Scotch, not the people and definitely not the whisky!

Sundays

Some places still hold Sunday as special, particularly on the Western Isles. You will find that there is no public transport and no shops open and some establishments will not let you arrive or depart on a Sunday. I have heard of places not letting you watch TV on a Sunday except for religious programmes and even the swings being chained up in the park. However strange this may appear in the 1990s, it is advisable to respect their wishes.

Addresses & Distances

Some addresses may include 'by' somewhere for instance 'by Lairg' or 'by Garve': beware, this does not mean they are close to that place, establishments can be up to 50 miles from their 'by' address.

Oh no, she mentioned the 'M' word!! I can hear it now from the Shetlands to Gretna Green, I will be cursed, cast out and ostracised. It seems to be an un-written law up here that we don't mention the midge (oh no, she did it again) to visitors especially if you work in tourism.

The theory is that if we all ignore the midges and never mention them in our guidebooks, they will simply go away... Wrong!! They are here, they are here to stay, and they are biting unsuspecting tourists even as I am writing this little piece. So, I intend to spill the beans, tell all and hopefully help you to avoid the midges or at least learn to live with them.

I do hope that you find this information useful, and even if you don't, it will give you something new to talk about at parties!

The combination of kilts and midges explain the origin of the Highland Fling (ha, ha). This well worn-out joke is no laughing matter, the midge is your worst nightmare. This tiny insect (related to the mosquito) is the curse of the summer in some parts of Scotland and even (I heard) as far down as the Lake District.

This wee creature with a wingspan of less than 1.4mm bites, relentlessly causing pain, itchiness, swelling and bloody misery to its victims. Midges recognise no social barriers and legend has it that Queen Victoria was half eaten by midges during a picnic in Sutherland.

In Scotland there are 34 known species of Midge but it is just one – Culicoides Impunctatus – which is deemed to be responsible for over 90% of all bites. Although it is the Highlands and Islands that are most 'famous' for their midges, there is no natural habitat or location in Scotland that is com-pletely midge free.

Not all midges bite – so it may be helpful to recognise the ones that do, it's quite simple; just look out for the blotches of dark flecked spots on their wings and the way they fold their wings scissor like – although this may prove a little impractical with the naked eye.

A reassuring note is that it is only the pregnant female that bites – male midges and non-pregnant females are herbivores!

The next paragraph is not for the faint-hearted, but I thought I'd slip it in for the more macabre among us.

Female midges hunt in packs and in a one hour period (if you were brave enough or daft enough to stay out that long), around 2,000 bites would take place. When the midge bites you, your skin is pierced by a pair of mandibles and maxillae with a scissor action cutting into the surface of the skin. When the wound is deep enough, blood is released from the victim's capillary vessels and the midge then rolls its mouth parts into a tube, enters into the wound and sucks the blood - if left undisturbed the midge will feed for 3 to 4 minutes.

Midgy Times

Tony has a theory that the number of midges is directly related to the number of visitors, ie.

lots of visitors = lots of midges

Although midges are around from May to mid-September, it is generally in July and August that they are at their worst. Midgies like damp, still and mild weather. Too much heat, wind or rain will deter them – midges are at their absolute worse on still evenings as the sun goes down.

Midges live for just 20-30 days during which time the female mates, then during the next 2 to 5 days must have a 'blood meal' before she lays her eggs... Then she starts all over again.

Midge Control

There are as many anti-midge remedies in Scotland as there are Scottish legends. Some work better than others and none is perfect. Be sure of one thing when shelling out your hard-earned for another commercial wonder-drug, female pregnant midges *have* to have a blood meal before they can lay their eggs. So if you are wearing the latest line in nasty smelling, foul tasting midge repellent and standing next to someone who is *not* using anything, the midge will bite your unprotected friend and not you. However, if you are *all* well protected she will endure the taste and the smell in her desperate need for blood and bite you anyway! So either walk between two unprotected friends or draw lots to see who's not going to be bitten today. I have heard that taking Brewers Yeast tablets for a couple of weeks before your visit can deter them. Tony assures me that drinking large quantities of organic beer while you are up here has the same effect – either that or you get so drunk you really don't care.

As a Vegan I can not be seen to recommend you to poison or splat natures creatures so my advice is simple – wear long trousers, long sleeves, a mask and a balaclava; or alternatively, visit us between September and June.

Our local radio Loch Broom FM became quite famous last year with its 'midge count' telling visitors when it was going to be a 'bad midge day'. The count became as vital as the weather forecast and the pollen count.

However annoying these wee beasties may be, I am sure they have some part to play in Nature's complex game. The grazing patterns of the deer are controlled by the midges as attacks force them further up the hills during summer. Midges are undoubtedly part of the food chain, and I'm sure that without the midge Scotland's diverse wildlife would be threatened in someway.

The midges are the guardians of Scotland and it wouldn't be the same without them (honest).

For more information, I recommend the book 'Midges in Scotland' by George Hendry published by Mercat Press, Edinburgh. (And see page 93!)

THE WEATHER

The Weather is the main topic of conversation from January until December, from one end of Scotland to the other. Rumours abound that it is always raining, always below freezing and always under seven foot of snow. So you may be surprised if you visit us and get wonderful clear sunny weather.

The only thing you can be sure of is that the weather is changeable and localised to the extreme – it can be raining at the front of our house and not at the back! There is a local saying that if you don't like the weather, just wait 'a wee whiley' and it will change. We often have all four seasons in one go and our barometer is permanently stuck on 'changeable'.

Basically December, January and February is winter – yes, it is cold and yes, generally we do get snow but the roads are usually cleared quickly and snow gates are in operation should the roads become impassable for a while. However severe the weather is, life goes on and the scenery is spectacular. To see the deer on the hills in thick snow is the stuff that 'Christmas cards' are made of. The only real problem is the dark: the further you go North, the less daylight hours there will be. (Yes, I know that's obvious, but it could be as few as five or six in late December so you need to make the most of them.)

The spring months of March & April can still be cold but generally not too bad and many think that May is the best time to visit – long clear days, no rain and no midges.

Don't let Scotland's wildlife go to the dogs...

The League Against Cruel Sports campaigns peacefully for an end to the barbarity of fox hunting and the coursing of live hares with dogs.

After years of hard work by the League, an Act of Parliament was passed in April 1996 that at last gave some protection to all wild mammals. But it is still legal to hunt a fox to exhaustion when it will be ripped apart by hounds or dug from its refuge by the terriermen. And it is still legal to set greyhounds onto the declining hare population in the name of sport.

To play your part in helping to abolish bloodsports, please return the tear-off form today.

LEAGUE
AGAINST CRUEL SPORTS

WORKING FOR WILDLIFE

First name _ _ _ _ _ _ _ Surname _ _ _ _ _ _ _ Mr/Mrs/Miss/Ms

Address _ _ _ _ _ _ _ _ _ _ _ _ _ _ _

☐ Please send information on the League's campaign to protect wildlife

☐ I enclose a donation to "LACS Ltd" for £ _ _ _ _ _ _

Please return this form to:

League Against Cruel Sports, 83-87 Union Street, London, SE1 1SG

Summer comes early and June gives us dark for just one or two hours between 1 AM and 3 AM then the sun is out again – it's fabulous. July and August can be very hot, sometimes too much so: mist, heat, crowds and midges are not everyone's cup of tea.

By September, things are cooling down and calming down, the crowds are gone and so have the midges, yet it is still quite often warm enough to head for the beach. Autumn is generally excellent weather for walking right through to November – but beware of the stalkers!.

A word of caution – dark comes quickly on the mountains and what starts off as a wee walk up a mountain can turn into a lesson in survival very quickly. Many people seem to spend fifty weeks of the year when their only exercise is the walk from the desk to the coffee machine, and then on holiday they think they are Chris Bonnington. Please take care, always let someone know where you are and when you will be back, leave a note on your car and always start back a good hour before you think you need to. Better still, join in with one of the organised walking/climbing groups – the local tourist board should be able to help you.

13

KEY TO FACILITIES

Serves Meat	M	Licensed	L
Serves Fish	F	Vegetarian/Vegan Proprietor	VP
Non Smoking	NS	Vegan Food Always Available	VA
Smoking Restricted Areas	SR	Vegan Food on Request	R
Meals for Non Residents	NR	Pets Welcome	P
Disabled Access	DA	Children Welcome	C
Disabled Facilities	DF	Veg. Cheese/Free Range Eggs	V
Special Diets	SD	Allergy/Pet Free Accomodation	A
Central Heating	CH	Environmental/Recycling Policy	E
En-Suite Rooms	ES	Exclusively Vegetarian/Vegan	J
Tea/Coffee Making Facililities	TC		

CHESTNUT HOUSE

Crosby Garrett
Kirkby Stephen
Cumbria
CA17 4PR
Tel: 017683 71230

Situated approximately half way between London & Fort William and 20 minutes from the M6 (junction 38) our cottage guest house in a tranquil village setting offers the ideal stopover for travellers between the south of England and the Highlands and Islands. Superb vegetarian/vegan evening meals and breakfasts; beautiful surrounding countryside. Who knows, next time you may want to stay a little longer

Brochure available.

Contact

Stephanie & John Dewhurst.

Sample Menus

Menus from around the world. All food home-made, including wholemeal and speciality breads.

Opening Times

All year

Prices (1996)

B&B £15.00. Evening Meal £9.00

Public Transport Details:

Station 5 miles – collection can be arranged.

Facilities

J, NS, SD, CH, VP, VR, P, C, V, E.

LANCRIGG VEGETARIAN COUNTRY HOUSE HOTEL

Easedale
Grassmere
Lake District
Tel: 015394 35317
Fax: 015394 38058

Quiet secluded setting half a mile from Grassmere Village. Historic house much loved by Lakeland poets and artists in 30 acres of private grounds. Four posters and whirlpool baths. Licensed. 3 Crowns commended.

Contact

Grant

Sample Menus

Grilled marinated peppers, aubergines, feta cheese and tomatoes. Parsnip and ginger soup, 3 nut loaf en-croute served with onion gravy, Spinach roulade. Chocolate pudding, blackberry pie, lemon pudding, homemade ice-cream.

Opening Times

All year

Prices

£40–£85 D+B&B. £19.50 dinner

Public Transport Details

Half a mile from Bus stop, Windermere. Train 15 minutes.

Facilities

J, SR, NR, DA, DF, SD, CH, ES, TC, L, VP, VA, P, C, A, V, E.

DUMFRIES & GALLOWAY, AND THE BORDERS

Dumfries & Galloway

Raiders from England came often over the Border, and visitors can today see the evidence including the 'Riding of the Marches' re-enacting the defence of the Scottish Realm.

The most famous place in Southern Scotland is 'Gretna Green', marriage place of so many runaway lovers. Even the most cynical among us just can't resist a visit to the 'Old Black Smith' Shop'. Those looking for beauty of a more natural kind can find it at 'The Devil's Beef Tub' (rather an unfortunate name but apparently it's lovely) and the 'Grey Mares Tail' near to Moffatt. On the coast there are miles of sandy beaches including Auchencairn which has a smugglers cave. Larger towns of Newton Stewart offer good shopping, Wanlockhead is Scotland's highest village and also home to the 'world gold panning championship's'. Whithorn can be dated back to 4000 BC – so you should try to fit in a visit to the standing stones at Torhousekie. There are many historic homes and an abundance of castles, most of which can be visited. Dumfries & Galloways was a place that Robbie Burns loved, so much so that most of his famous works were penned here.

The 'Isle of Whithorn' is in Dumfries and Galloway and in days gone by, visitors would be relieved of their money to be taken 'across' to this island only to find on their arrival it is not an island at all!

The Borders

The Borders are alive with the history of the many battles (most with the English) and in fact the heart of Robert the Bruce lies buried at Melrose; but there is also some of the most beautiful scenery. Only 1000 people live in the Borders and probably as a result there is a multitude of wildlife including red deer, wild goats and the golden eagle.

The Gulf Stream ensures there is a mild climate and therefore beautiful gardens are everywhere, particularly at Priorwood and Kailzie

The Borders offer a very special service for children, just call the tourist board with the ages of your kids and they will recommend places for them to visit which I am sure will include Harestanes near Jedburgh which has woodland walks and a games room.

DON'T MISS! *Burn's House, Gretna Green, Galloway Forest Park and the Standing Stones of Torhousekie.*

Dumfries & Galloway Tourist Board	Scottish Borders Tourist Board
Campbell House	Tourist Information Centre
Bankend Road	Murray's Green
Dumfries	Jedburgh
DG1 4TH	TD8 6BE
Tel: 01387 250434	Tel: 01835 863435
Fax: 01387 250462	Fax: 01835 864099

Health Food Shops

Newton Stewart Health Food Shop
18/20 Queen Street,
Newton Stewart
01671 402023

Sunrise Wholefoods
49 King Steet,
Castle Douglas
01556 253761

the Silent ark

By Juliet Gellatley
with Tony Wardle

a chilling exposé of meat – the global killer

Published by Thorsons at £6.99

Juliet Gellatley's hard-hitting personal story is riveting, bold and persuasive. She exposes the political protection, disinformation and PR glitz which have propped up an all-powerful meat culture. Some in the industry have called her 'public enemy number 1'.

"We are destroying the planet, impoverishing the world's poor and destroying our own health in pursuit of something we don't even need. The tool for this destruction is our abuse of billions of diseased and dejected farm animals. This is a brave and important book which will be seen as a classic." Michael Mansfield QC

Serialised in The Times.

"This is the ultimate argument for a vegetarian and vegan world and is told with great skill... a classic." The Vegan Magazine

"An impassioned and thought-provoking plea for action from the founder of Viva! and one of the country's most vocal vegetarian campaigners." BBC Vegetarian Good Food

"Powerful, persuasive, alarming." Peter Martin, Mail on Sunday

"A gripping story of discovery which makes you want to keep turning the pages..." Nicky Campbell Show, BBC Radio 1

"An immensely readable expose; buy it!" Joyce D'Silva, CIWF

"Passion backed by science... Controversial and powerful..." Manchester Evening News

"The Silent Ark is hard to put down. Juliet Gellatley's first-hand knowledge jumps from the page and hits you in the stomach... very persuasive." Alison Page, Red Pepper Magazine

Available from good bookshops or direct from *Viva!*
Send £6.99 plus 70p p&p (payable to *Viva!*) to:
Viva!, PO Box 212, Crewe CW1 4SD
Or order by credit card on 01270 522500.

Viva!

Registered Charity No. 1037486

1. ABBEY COTTAGE

26 Main Street
Dumfries
New Abbey
DG2 8BY
Tel: 01387 850377

Contact

Morag McKie/Jackie Wilson

Restaurant/Coffee Shop and Craft Shop

Sample Menus

Lunch: Cauliflower/mushroom soup

Ploughman's with local vegetables and cheese.

Opening Times

10.00am – 5.30pm seven days

April – October and weekends in November and December.

Public Transport Details

Public bus service from Dumfries to Solway Coast – passing through New Abbey.

Facilities

M, NS, DA, DF, SD, CH, L, VA, C, V, E

2. THE ROSSAN

Auchencairn
Dumfries DG17 1QR
Tel: 01556 649 269

The Rossan is an early Victorian ex-Manse on the eastern edge of Auchencairn. The Rossan is for you, especially if you find an abundance of books and pictures more congenial than doilies and ornaments. There is no sitting room, though guests can linger at the table if they wish, as the bedrooms – each with home-made patchwork quilts – are meant to serve as bed sitters. Views are of the acre of garden or Auchencairn Bay and the Cumbrian hills. This is also a great area for fortifications – Celtic, Roman, mediaeval. Clothes dried overnight, dogs allowed in house, on lead. 10% discount Vegetarian Society Members. STB Approved.

Bring your own alcohol.

Contact

Mrs Bardsley

Sample Menus

No such thing as a typical dinner, soup, stuffed tomatoes, and home made ice-cream etc. We provide organically grown fruit & vegetables from the garden in season. Gluten Free diets are always available and diabetics are given sympathetic assistance.

Opening Time

Feb–Dec

Prices

B&B £14. D+B&B £22.

Public Transport Details

20 miles from Dumfries

Facilities

M, F, NS, DF, SD, CH, TC, VP, VA, P, V, E,

See Map on Page 49

3. EARTHWARD

Tweed Horizons
Newton St Boswells
Roxburghshire
TD6 0SG
Tel: 01835 822122
Fax: 01835 822199

Project for promotion of a healthier eating in Scotland. Demonstrations, Courses, Public Participation and Client-Specific Design Exercises.

Fresh chemical free fruit and vegetables in season – only what we grow!

Contact

Mark Buxton

Opening Times

9–5pm weekdays

Public Transport Details

Bus to Newton St Boswells from Edinburgh Carlisle, Berwick or locally.

4. GREY GABLES

Springwood Road
Peebles
Borders
EH45 9HB
Tel: 01721 721252

Old coach house, in quiet area but within easy walking distance of Peebles. Totally renovated with pleasant gardens and off road parking. 1 double, 1 twin . 1 double and 1 twin. Many places locally to get evening meal.

Contact

Sue Isherwood

Sample Menus

Breakfast: home-made muesli, fresh fruits, different everyday.

Cooked breakfast - home-made veggie sausages, cutlets, eggs etc. Home-made breads and pancakes

Vegetarian biryani & accompaniments.

Home made ice creams & fruit puddings.

Opening Times

Easter to End September.

Prices

2 course dinner – £5
B&B £15. D+B&B £22

Public Transport Details

Hourly bus service to Edinburgh – 10 minutes walk away.

Hourly bus service to Galashiels, Melrose & connections to other Border towns.

Facilities

SD, CH, TC, VP, VA, V, E.

AYRSHIRE & ARAN, EDINBURGH & LOTHIAN, GLASGOW & THE CLYDE

Ayrshire

Ayrshire has fabulous beaches, lively resorts towns, peaceful villages and golf courses. Nature lovers come here for the wildlife, outdoor folk for the water sports, trekking and cycling. You can also visit the birth place of Robert Burns or go in search of the legends of the Vikings.

Aran

An unspoilt and peaceful island meant for recreation and relaxation. Aran is described as Scotland in miniature, it has mountains, glens and woodlands. Aran also has a diverse selection of festivals – drama, folk and music.

East, West and Mid-Lothian

In the heart of Scotland, and in the heart of its history – prehistoric earth dwellings, hill forts, ancient monuments and dramatic castles. Walkers of all abilities will find happiness here. In West Lothian there is Limlithgow Palace, birth place of Mary Queen of Scots and James V. There are 40 miles of coastline in East Lothian including Gullane and Belhaven bay which have won 'seaside awards' for clean sand and clean water. Dunbar has been recorded as the sunniest and driest town in Scotland for over 30 years.

Edinburgh

I don't know what I can say about Edinburgh that hasn't been said by people more qualified than me, so...

For what it's worth, Edinburgh is Scotland's capital and – in my humble opinion – it is the most beautiful city in the world. Edinburgh castle is the centre piece of a city which just seems to have the right balance between bustling shops, theatres and clubs, all in a natural setting. It even has sandy beaches and the sea. It is also a good city for pubs with over 700 of them, there are theatres to rival London's West End and whenever you go, I'm sure there will be a festival of some kind going on. Beyond the well known Edinburgh festival in August, there are also festivals of folk music, animation, science, children's theatre, etc.

Glasgow

Glasgow is one of Europe's most vibrant culture capitals and host to the finest range of fine art, museums, galleries, with an all year round programme of entertainment. The architect will notice Medieval and Victorian buildings as well as the art nouveau style of Charles Rennie Mackintosh. You can 'shop till you drop' then take a rest in one of the many cafe bars. At night, a lot of pubs offer live entertainment of comedy, music, dance or a traditional Ceilidh.

Go just a little further afield to greater Glasgow, and you can relax in the countryside and the many parks and gardens. You will agree that the name Glasgow justifies its Gaelic translation of 'dear green place' (or was that green deer place?). Day cruises set sail from Gourock on the firth of Clyde and Anderston Quay. The town of Paisley (world famous for its pattern) has the fabulous Paisley Abbey and the Thomas Coats memorial church – a shining example of Gothic Architecture.

Clyde Valley

New Lanark was one of the largest cotton mill complexes in the world and today you can relive that time in the 'Annie Mcleod Experience'. Wordsworth and Dickens visited this area and no doubt took inspiration from the Falls of Clyde – Corra Linn and Bonnington Linn – which are now part of a Scottish Wildlife Trust Reserve. Blantyre remembers Dr David Livingstone (I presume) and Biggar boasts 'London is big, but Biggar is bigger!' - not in size maybe, but four museums depict 'big' history and on New Year's Eve, Biggar hosts the largest bonfire in Scotland.

 Edinburgh Castle, Paisley Abbey, Annie Mcleod Experience and the Time Capsule.

Ayrshire & Aran Tourist Board
Burns House
Burn's Statue Square
Ayr KA7 1UP
Tel: 01292 262555
Fax: 01292 269555

Greater Glasgow and Clyde Valley
Tourist Board
39 St Vincent Place
Glasgow G1 2ER
Tel: 0141 204 4480
Fax: 0141 204 4772

Edinburgh & Lothian Tourist Board
Edinburgh Information Centre
3 Princes Street
Edinburgh   EH2 2QP
Tel: 0131 557 1700
Fax: 0131 557 5118

Health Food Shops

- **Blackhall Health & Wholefoods**
11 Marischal Place, Edinburgh
0131 315 2005
- **Food for Thought**
13 Hardgate, Haddington
01620 823196
- **Good Food**
255 Morningside Road, Edinburgh
0131 452 9020
- **Natures Larder**
99 High Street, North Berwick
01620 895383
- **The Health Food Shop.**
32 Bank Street, Galashiels
01896 758085
- **Hanover Health Food.**
40 Hanover Street, Edinburgh
0131 225 4291
- **Kelso Wholefoods.**
52 Wood Market, Kelso
01573 225664
- **Millars of Morningside.**
414 Morningside Road, Edinburgh
0131 447 2468
- **The Millstone.**
276b High Street, Linlithgow
01506 847270
- **The New Leaf.**
20 Argyle Place, Edinburgh
0131 228 8840
- **Hendersons Farm Shop.**
92 Hanover Street, Edinburgh
0131 225 6694
- **The Granary**
34 Busby Road, Clarkston, Glasgow
0141 638 0001
- **Evergreen Wholefoods**
136, Nithsdale Road, Glasgow G41
0141 422 1303
- **Forrest & Niven Health Food**
73, St Vincent Street, Glasgow
0141 221 7865
- **Forrest & Niven Health Food**
27 Townhead Street, Glasgow
01698 281415
- **Grassroots**
48, Woodlands Road, Charing Cross,
Glasgow
0141 353 3278

- **Health & Herbs**
Unit 19, In Shops, The Paisley Centre,
23 High Street, Paisley
0141 848 5312
- **A3 Health Shop**
20a Ritchie Street,
West Kilbride KA23 9EL
01294 829656
- **Sundrum Organics**
Home Delivery/Mail Order
01290 552020
- **Airdrie Grain & Halth Foods**
37, Hallcraig Street, Airdrie
01236 754291
- **The Natural Body**
44 Wellgate, Lanark
01555 661400
- **The Village Shop**
Stone Road, Whiting Bay, Aran
01770 700349
- **Good Food Shop**
Auchannie Road, Brodick
01771 302427
- **The Grain Store**
16, John Wood Street, Port Glasgow
01475 742721
- **Quality Deli and Health Foods**
123, Douglas Street, Glasgow
0141 331 2984
- **Simply Healthy**
14, Skirving Street, Glasgow, G41
0141 632 0664
- **Sundrum Organics**
Home Delivery/Mail Order
01290 552020
- **Wholefood Harvest**
8 Main Street, Strathaven
01357 522605
- **Health Food & Grain Store**
11, Canon Way, Cumbernauld
01236 726766
- **Pure Necessities**
713, Gt Western Road, Glasgow
0141 339 2669
(Juice, Vitamins & Minerals only)

Hi, I'm Uri Geller

and boy, am I glad to be vegan! What with BSE in dairy cattle, salmonella in chicken and eggs, the threat of a yield-promoting hormone (BST) in milk, listeria in some soft cheeses — not to mention the high, artery-clogging saturated fat content of fibre-lacking dairy foods and eggs — and who knows what other health hazards still to be uncovered — it has never been a better time to take that next small step to becoming animal-free.

So, if you're looking for peace of mind, good health, and enough energy to join me in my 50 miles-a-day cycling routine, simply send two-first class stamps to my friends at the Vegan Society. They'll be pleased to help you on your way!

THE
Vegan
SOCIETY

Promoting a diet free of animal products for the benefit of people, animals and the environment

The Vegan Society, Dept SG, Donald Watson House, 7 Battle Road, St Leonards-on-Sea, East Sussex TN37 7AA (Tel. 01424 427393)

5. HENDERSONS SALAD TABLE

94 Hanover Street
Edinburgh
EH2 1DR
Tel: 0131 225 2131
Fax: 0131 220 3542

Basement café and restaurant, an institution of vegetarian food.

Contact

Duty Manager

Sample Dishes

Spinach & Barley Soup. Veggie Haggis with clapshot. Stuffed aubergine with wild/oyster mushroom sauce. Curried parsnip bake. Banana & tofu cheesecake. Fruit crumbles.

Opening Times

8am–10.45pm Monday–Saturday
Sundays 9am–9pm during Festival.

Facilities

J, SD, L, VP, VA, VR, C, V

6. DAVID MURRAY

1 Gayfield Place
Edinburgh
EH7 4AB
Tel: 0131 557 4752

Top floor of classical Edinburgh building. No lift but good views. Ten minutes walk from train/bus station and Princes street.

Contact

David Murray

Sample Breakfast Menu

Potato scones, mushrooms, vegan sausage, tomatoes, beans, cereals, local bread, fruit juice.

Opening Times

All year

Prices

£20–£25 per person per night.

Public Transport Details

Bus stop Elin Row 7, 10, 11, 12, 14, 16, 17, 22, 25, 55, 87, 88

Facilities

J, NS, CH, ES, TC VP, VA, V, E

7. SIX MARY'S PLACE

Raeburn Place
Edinburgh
Stockbridge
EH16 1JD
Tel: 0131 332 8965
Fax: 0131 539 7375

Three storey Georgian townhouse in fashionable Stockbridge area. Bedrooms individually decorated, antiques, dining conservatory, restful gardens. Georgian lounge with TV tea & coffee making facilities in all bedrooms and centrally heated throughout.

Contact

Elaine Gale

Sample Menus

Vegetarian sausage, mushrooms, tomatoes, eggs, home-made potato cakes, Aubergine & cheese bake served with green vegetables and potatoes. Cashew nut roast with apricot stuffing, served with red pepper sauce, baked mushrooms and potatoes.

Opening Times

All year

Public Transport Details

Regular bus service from Raeburn Place, into city centre (10 minutes) and return bus service every 20 minutes.

Facilities:

J, NS, NR, SD, CH, ES, TC, VR, C, V, A, E.

8. PROSPECT BANK HOUSE

16 Prospect Bank Road
Edinburgh
EH6 7NS
Tel: 0131 553 3558

Bed and breakfast in lovely family home, circ. 1725 in the Leith area of Edinburgh. Vegetarian/Vegan breakfast with an emphasis on healthy and exciting organic home-made food. Extensive knowledge and understanding of special diets, including food combining. Beautiful rooms, large comfortable beds and bathrooms with pedestal baths.

Contact

Morag McCulloch

Sample Menus

Breakfast: Home-made organic banana bread, organic cous cous cake and blueberry fruit spread, wholemeal croissants and organic breads. Organic porridge. Fresh fruits with sheep's yoghurt and maple syrup. Crepes, smoothies etc. etc. Herb/organic tea and organic decaf. Coffee.

Opening Times

All year except Christmas.

Prices

£17.50–£20 per person per night.

Public Transport Details

Various bus routes into city centre, 15 mins. approximately.

Facilities

J, NS, SD, CH, TC, VR, C, V, E.

9. UBIQUITOUS CHIP

12 Ashton Lane
Glasgow
Tel: 0141 334 5007
Fax: 0141 337 1302

Main restaurant open seven days a week for both lunch and dinner. Upstairs restaurant remains open all day for a simple snack, coffee or substantial but informal meal.

The Chip Wine Shop situated next to the restaurant is nationally acclaimed for quality range and value for money.

Vouchers to any value are available from the restaurant and maybe redeemed in any of our outlets.

We also operate an excellent outside catering service which can cope with anything from informal buffets to dinners on the grand scale.

Contact

S. Wilson

Sample Menus

Homemade soup. Wild mushroom and pearl barley risotto. A flan of chargrilled courgettes with a plum sauce.Homemade ice-cream, carrot cake.

Opening Times

Upstairs Restaurant 12–11pm

Main Restaurant 12–2.30pm & 5.30–11pm

Prices

Main courses £5–£10

Two courses & coffee £26

Public Transport Details

Directly behind Hillhead Underground Station.

Facilities

M, F, DA, DF, L, VR, C, E.

10. JANET ANDERSON

East Lochhead
Largs Road, Lochwinnoch
Renfrewshire PA12 4DX
Tel/Fax: 01505 842610
Mobile: 08585 565131

Situated within Clyde Muirshiel Regional Park, overlooking Barr Loch and the Renfrewshire hills, yet only 15 mins from Glasgow Airport. Close to a nature reserve and watersports facilities, the Paisley–Irvine cycle track passes the house.

Three self-catering cottages converted from former byres overlook a courtyard. Two cottages sleep 6, and one sleeps 2. Short breaks available except during high season.

Two B&B bedrooms overlooking garden and Barr Loch. 1 Twin with private bathroom, 1 Family/Double en suite.

Sample Menus

Home produced free range eggs, vegetables and honey. Breakfast: mushroom herb burgers, omelette, parmesan potato cakes and apple & raisin muffins. Dinner: home made soups. Broccoli and cheese roulade with red pepper sauce.Aubergine and tomato gallette,Banoffee pie, fresh fruit salad or poached vanilla pears.

Packed lunches made to order.

Opening Times

All year

Prices

6 berth cottage £160–£310 per week (Saturday - Saturday)
2 berth cottage £130–£205 per week.
B&B £25 per person

Public Transport Details

Train station 2 miles ahead

Facilities

DF, TC, NS, C, CH,

Welcome Host, Credit Cards accepted

BENJAMIN ZEPHANIAH

PREFERS

Plamil

TO UDDER MILK

NEW SUPER TASTING

The EC Management Committee for Milk and Milk products has ruled that the name soya milk must discontinue and the Government new approved name "Soya non dairy alternative to milk" will be gradually phased in (the name Soya milk will still be around in 1997)

RANGE IN HEALTH STORES INCLUDES:

Soya 'milks'	Egg-free mayonnaise
Rice puddings	Chocolate bars
Carob bars	Organic chocolates
Carob spreads	Organic chocolate drops
Carob drops	Veeze

---

11. ISLE OF ARAN DISTILLERIES

Lochranza
Isle of Arran
Tel: 01770 830 264
Fax: 01770 830 611

Distillery Visitor Centre

Guided Tours

Shop

Audio visual, exhibition and restaurant
(opening Spring 1997).

Contact

Gillian McCreadie

Opening Times

10.00am - 6.00pm - 7 days.

Prices

Tours/Audio Visual display £2.50.

Public Transport Details

Buses to Lochranza.

Facilities

V,E,

❋ *5% discount to readers of this guide*

Key to Facilities is on Page 13

PERTHSHIRE, FIFE, ANGUS & DUNDEE

Perthshire

Perth is a former Scottish capital and as such has a wealth of historic associations; it also has a tradition of extending a warm welcome to all its visitors. Pitlochry is a bustling resort famous for its theatre and ideal for sports lovers. Aberfeldy has Perthshire's highest mountain, largest loch and longest glen.

Fife

The Kingdom of Fife is so called because Dumfermline was Scotland's royal capital for 500 years. Fife offers a combination of history, leisure facilities, natural beauty and friendliness. North East Fife seems to get the best of any good weather that is going and rainfall is low (compared to the rest of Scotland that is, not the Sahara). Famous Fife people include Adam Smith – author of 'Wealth of Nations' – and novelist and historian John Buchan. Kinghorn is the place for water sports, Leven for the seaside, and Kirkcaldy for shopping.

Angus

Angus covers the coastline North of Tay to the Grampian mountains. It is one of the most important parts of Scotland for influence and history. The venue of the battle of Nechtansmere between Pictish warriers and the Northumbrians in 685 AD became the centre of Pictish power on their victory. There are many examples of Pictish symbol stones and gravestones at St Vigeans museum and Aberlemno.

Following Robert the Bruce's victory at Bannockburn in 1320, the 'declaration of Arbroath' was signed at Arbroath Abbey confirming Scotland's independence!

Angus has miles upon miles of quiet beaches and beautiful countryside. The Angus glens are a must if you are a walker, a botanist or a photographer.

Dundee

Dundee on the North bank of the River Tay is one of Scotland's smallest cities and was a settlement from pre-Roman times, as well as a site of many battles with the English – William (Braveheart) Wallace was educated here.

Today, Dundee is a thriving tourist area with excellent shopping, entertainment and heritage sites.

The sea bought trade and prosperity to Dundee. Fortunes were made from the three J's – jam, jute and journalism. At one point, Dundee had more millionaires per head than any other city in Great Britain.

Dundee is perfect for short breaks at any time of the year. On summer evenings, 'ghost -walks' are held through the city. Climb up the hill known as 'Dundee Law' and you will find out why the Iron Age people chose this spot to build their fort. Today you can see two Tay bridges, the Fife coastline, the Angus Glens and the Highlands of Perthshire.

DON'T MISS! *Discovery Quay, J M Barrie's house*

Perthshire Tourist Board
Administrative Headquarters
Lower City Mills
West Mill Street
Perth PH1 5QP
Tel: 01738 627958
Fax: 01738 630416

Angus & City of Dundee Tourist Board
4 City Square
Dundee
DD1 3BA
Tel: 01382 434664
Fax: 01382434665

Kingdom of Fife Tourist Board
7 Hanover Court
Glenrothes
Fife KY7 5SB
Tel: 01592 750066
Fax: 01592 611180

Health Food Shops

• **Health Food Store**
 2 Whitehouse Avenue, Kirkcaldy
01592 266651
• **Paganinis**
10 Perth Road, Dundee
01382 228574
• **Good Health**
16 King Street, Crieff
01764 653706
• **The Granary**
8 Queen Street, Carmoustie
01241 855272
• **Highland Health Store**
7 & 16 St John Street, Perth
01738 628102
• **Libra Wholefoods**
183 South Street, St Andrews
01334 475552
• **Tayside Health Foods
& Vegetarian Deli**
40-44 Commercial Street, Dundee
01382 201660

Vegetarian/Vegan Contact
Val Watson
c/o Dundee Wholefoods
10 Perth Road
Dundee
Tel: 01382 645297

12. SUNFLOWER COFFEE SHOP

39 Whytescauseway
Nr. The High Street
Kirkcaldy
Fife
Tel: 01592 646266
Fax: 01592 646266

Contact

Linda Butcher

Sample Menus

All day vegetarian breakfast, stovies, aubergine & tomato bake, cashew & tarragon rissoles, mushroom bridies, shepherdess pie, spicy beanfeast, chocolate Amaretto cheesecake, toffee apple cake. Selection of deliciously different filled rolls.

Opening Time

8.30am–4.30pm Monday–Saturday.

Prices

Snacks & meals £1.35–£2.50
Cakes 65p–£1.40

Facilities

J, NS, DA, DF, VP, VA, C, V

Organic Wines

29

Over 100 organic wines, juices, beers and ciders, many Vegetarian Society approved
Better for you **and** the environment

Trade and Mail Order supplied

List from **Vinceremos**
261 Upper Town St, Leeds LS13 3JT

0113 257 7545

DELTA MasterCard VISA

Scotland-wide delivery

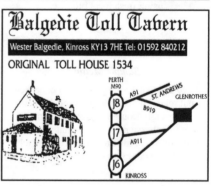

Balgedie Toll Tavern

Wester Balgedie, Kinross KY13 7HE Tel: 01592 840212

ORIGINAL TOLL HOUSE 1534

PERTH M90 | A91 | ST. ANDREWS | GLENROTHES | B919 | J8 | J7 | A911 | J6 | KINROSS

THE ROSSAN

Perfect for touring Galloway, birdwatching, painting and riding
Mr & Mrs Bardsley • Tel. 01556 640269

INVERDEEN HOUSE B&B

Ballater – Royal Deeside AB35 5QJ
Tel. Sandy Munroe 013397 55759

See Map on Page 49

13. BALGEDIE TOLL TAVERN

Wester Balgedie
Kinross
KY13 7HE
Tel: 01592 840 212

Old Toll House Inn of character 1534 specialising in vegetarian and low fat dishes as well as traditional Scottish fayre using fresh local produce.

Contact

Jocelyn Glebocki

Sample Menus

Vegetable pates - various.Carrot & cashew nut roast. Hazelnut & vegetable burgers. Vegetable Bourgignon & dumplings. Broccoli cheese melts. White nut roast with herb stuffing. Pitta breads - various snacks. Clootie dumplings. Yoghurt & ices, meringues etc.

Opening Times

7 days 11am–3pm & 6pm–11pm

Prices

3 course lunch £8–£10

evening 3 course dinner £12.95

Public Transport Details

Local bus route.

Facilities

M, F, SR, NR, DA, SD, L, VR, C, V, E

14. GLENRANNOCH HOUSE

Kinloch Rannoch
Perthshire
PH16 5QA
Tel: 01882 632 307

Vegetarian Guest House and former manse is situated on the edge of beautiful Kinloch Rannock. We have a large organic fruit and vegetable area and free renge hens enjoy life at the bottom of the garden.

Contact

Margarate Legate

Sample Menus

Breakfast: Organic porridge, prunes, American pancakes, maple syrup, own free range eggs, home-made organic bread.

Dinner: Aubergine frites, broccoli roulade and red pepper sauce, poached plums with cinnamon cream.

Opening Times

January–December (Closed Christmas)

Prices

B&B £17–£18

D+B&B £29–£30

Public Transport Details

Bus from Pitlochry twice daily, trains & buses from Pitlochry to Edinburgh, London & Inverness.

Facilities

J, NS, NR, SD, CH, WHB, VP, VR, P, C, V, A, E

ARGYLL, LOCH LOMOND, STIRLING, THE TROSSACHS, MULL, BUTE, IONA & OBAN

The Scottish Tourist Board saw fit to lump together Argyll, Loch Lomond, Stirling, The Trossachs and some eleven islands into one tourist board, which means that they now have the dubious privilege of being the tourist board with the longest name. Luckily for them they also have some of the most amazing places:

Loch Lomond

Loch Lomond is known as the queen of Scotland's Lochs, it has woods, bays and clear blue waters. An 18th century Jacobite prisoner penned 'I'll take the high road' in fond memory of his beautiful home town.

Stirling

It was said that to 'hold Stirling' was to 'hold Scotland' and as proof of that there are seven battlefields surrounding Stirling. William (Braveheart) Wallace led his army to victory on a battle site near Stirling and it was probably for this reason that Stirling was chosen for the European première of 'Braveheart'. Mel Gibson was heard to say "I've never had such a welcome – I've never seen anything like it", so if it's good enough for Mel...

Oban

Oban means 'little bay' in Gaelic. It is one of Scotland's most popular holiday towns, it has numerous golf courses and is also the 'unofficial' capital of the West Highlands. The Victorians left their mark on Oban, the most famous building is McCaigs tower which was built about a hundred years ago and kept unemployed stonemasons in work right up until McCaigs' death and was therefore never finished. Oban is also gateway to the Isles – Lismore, Mull, Iona, Coll, Colonsay and Tiree.

The Trossachs

The Trossachs is the frontier country where the Highlands meet the Lowlands and is said to be a miniature Highlands. It was also the domain of the infamous brigand Rob Roy McGregor.

Islay & Tiree *(The Inner Hebrides)*

Islay is a tranquil and enchanting island at the southern end of the Hebrides. Historical associations dates back to Neolithic times and it caters for a diverse range of interests. The Islay malt whisky is here too!

Tiree is known as the Sunshine Island, it has beautiful beaches, rare birds and is ideal for windsurfing.

Bute   *by Mandy King, Bute House Hotel*

Bute is Scotland's first Island in the Highlands, is within easy access of the mainland (20 minutes by ferry) and is host to three lively music festivals – Jazz (May 2–6), Folk (July19–22) and Country (September 27–29).

Nature lovers will enjoy this 'Scotland in miniature', with its high wild ground in the North, a central lowland belt and tamer hill ground in the South. This makes for a wide variety of habitat, with corresponding number of birds and mammals. There are 5 freshwater lochs all of fairly easy access. Deer are commonly spotted and the resident colony of seals allow you to get quite close to them. Surrounded by the gulf stream, Bute also hosts a great number of plants, not to mention a number of palm trees. Yachts and pleasure-boats moor in the new purpose built marina.

Rothesay castle, once home to Scottish kings, is in the town centre. Visit Celtic standing stones at Ettric Bay or an Iron Age fort at Dunagoil. More recent, Mount Stuart House and Gardens are open May to September: this high Victorian Gothic house of stunning architectural detail stands in 300 acres of woodland, offering walks and peaceful sites. The house was winner of the Scottish Tourism Oscar for 1995.

Rothesay winter garden has a small cinema, bistro and function room where dance classes, discos, fitness programs and functions are held. There are many lively bars around the island so there's something for everyone.

Mull   *by Heather Heald, Bruach Mhor*

Fionnphort is at the western end of the Rass of Mull, a hilly, wild and rocky peninsula in the South of Mull. We have splendid coastal scenery and fine walks. Many boat trips are on offer:

- 5-minute ferry to Iona (where St Columba landed in 563);
- Half-day trips to Staffa, a spectacular island made of columnar basalt, housing a small but friendly colony of puffins and also Fingals cave;
- Day trips to Lunga, where there are colonies of puffins, razorbills, guillemots, kittiwakes and others.

You will almost certainly see seals on these trips and it's fairly likely you will see porpoises or dolphins; many people have seen whales too.

From the hill behind Bruach Mhor, you can see the Islands of Jura, Colonsay, Islay, Iona, Staffa, The Treshrush Isles, Tiree, Coll, Rhum, Canna and very occasionally Skye and Barra.

The Rass of Mull has many sandy beaches, some close to the road and some several miles walk. Even in the height of summer, you stand a good chance of being the only one there. There is some great hill-walking in the middle of the Island and a great climb to the top of Ben More, our only Munro.

Iona   *by Ewan Mathers, Iona Cottage*

Iona is a small Scottish Island of great natural beauty and spiritual interest. It is also a well-known centre of Earth-energies and ancient Druid activity. More recently Iona became a focus for Christianity in the Western Isles. Following Columba's arrival from Ireland in 563 AD, the Abbey and the Nunnery were built in the 13th century. In 1938, George Macleod founded the Iona Community which rebuilt the Abbey.

It has unique local geology (with rocks older than life itself), fantastic flora and fauna (including wild Orchids and the rare Sea Holly), and rich bird life (ranging from the rare, elusive Corncrake of the summer months to flocks of Curlews in the winter).

DON'T MISS! *Inverary Jail, Stirling Castle, Dunollie Castle, Mount Stuart House and Rothesay Castle.*

Argyll, The Isles, Loch Lomond,
Stirling and Trossachs Tourist Board
7 Alexander Place
Dunoon
Argyll
PA23 8AB

Health Food Shops

- **Stirling Health Food Store**
  29 Dumbarton Road, Stirling
  01786 464903
- **Wholefood Centre**
  83, Argyll Street, Dunoon
  01369 703892
- **Eco Grainstore**
  50 Hillfoot Street, Dunoon
  01369 705103
- **The Grapevine**
  49 Victoria Street, Rothesay, Bute
  01700 504414
- **Healthcraft**
  62 West Princes Street,
  Helensburgh
  01436 674993

argyll hotel
isle of iona

A delightful friendly hotel, on the beautiful
Island of Iona.

Cosy lounges with open fires, spacious dining
room, sunlounge. Cottagey bedrooms with
electric blankets, kettles, etc. We serve
excellent home cooking using home-grown
vegetables, and vegetarian meals using
wholefoods. Residents' licence. Recommended
in many leading hotel guides.

Argyll Hotel, Isle of Iona PA76 6SJ
Tel. 01681 700334 • Fax. 01681 700328

15. BUTE HOUSE HOTEL

**4 West Princess Street
Rothesay
Isle of Bute
PA20 9AF
Tel: 01700 502481
Fax: 01700 505117**

Attractive Victorian hotel, 2 minutes from
the harbour in central Rothesay. A Warm
welcome awaits you. Comfortable rooms
with all modern private facilities. Licensed
restaurant serving good fresh fruits,
carefully prepared. Candlelit dinners
overlooking the harbour and bay.

Contact
Mandy King

Sample Menus
Breakfast – Continental/cereals, toast, rolls,
fruit juice, fresh fruit, beverages.

Dinner: (Vegan) Vegetable spring rolls &
oriental dipping sauce.

Tofu Satay with rice and aubergine in
hoisin sauce

Melon & ginger island dream with fruits of
the Orient

Opening Times
April–October

Prices
£15–£24 B&B per person per night.
£7–£15 Dinner

Public Transport Details
From Glasgow; train to Wemyss Bay-ferry,
Wemyss Bay to Rothesay less than 2 hours.

Facilities
**F, NS, NR, SD, CH, WHB, TC, L, VP,
VA, C, A**

16. AN TAIRBEART HERITAGE CENTRE

Tarbert
Loch Fyne
Argyll
PA29 6SX
Tel: 01880 820190
Fax: 01880 820042

An Tairbeart provides a shop window for Argyll & the Islands' superb fresh produce. Tastings and cookery demonstrations are an important part of a varied programme of events, which includes green woodworking, spinning, ceilidhs, etc. Guided walks explore the abundant wild food and traditional herbal remedies as well as the areas' rich natural and folk history. Efforts are made to stock the shop with goods from local and sustainable sources.

Contact

Alison Sykora

Food

Manager Alison Sykora who formerly ran the popular Smiddy in Lochgilphead, designs imaginative menus at An Tairbeart which always include vegetarian and vegan dishes. Special diets can be catered for with prior notice

Directions

Two minutes south of Tarbert on main A83 Campbeltown road.

17. BRUACH MHOR

Fionnphort
Isle of Mull
PA66 6BL
Tel: 01681 700276
Fax: 01681 700276

Bruach Mhor is a modernised, centrally heated crofthouse standing alone on the slopes of Tor Mor, a hill just north of Fionnphort _ mile from the 5 minute ferry to the Isle of Iona. We take pride in serving wholesome and delicious breakfasts and dinners using home-grown organic vegetables whenever possible.

Contact

Heather Heald

Sample Menus

Breakfast: home-made yoghurt, fresh fruit, prunes and apricots, home-made oatcakes, lentil and apple burgers, mushrooms etc.

Herb & fruit teas. Packed lunch, humus and salad sandwiches, home made fruitcake.

Dinner: Pea and mint, leek & lemon soup. Bean casseroles, red dragon pie, quiches, nut roads, stir fries, frozen fruit yoghurt.

Opening Times

January–December (except Christmas and New Year)

Prices

B& B £15. Dinner £10.

Packed Lunch £3

Transport Details

Caledonian MacBrayne ferry from Oban or Lochaline Tel 01631 562285

Buses connect with most ferries,

By car, turn left off the ferry, follow A849 to Fionnphort (37 miles).

Facilities

M, F, SD, CH, WHB, TC, VA, C, V, E

18. IONA COTTAGE

Isle of Iona, Argyll
PA76 6SJ
Tel: 01681 700 579

Iona is a small Scottish island of great natural historical and spiritual interest. It is also a well known centre of Earth-energies and ancient Druid activity. Iona Cottage is a recently renovated 200 year old croft house standing on a shallow rise facing the jetty. We have three guest bedrooms and an open fire in the sitting-room. Guests share their meals in the sun lounge overlooking the Sound of Iona.

Contact

Hester Machin. Ewan Mathers

Sample Menus

Breakfast: home-made bread and yoghurt, enormous fruit bowl, varying cooked breakfast with free range eggs.

Packed lunches: home-made quiche, humus, cheese, salad sandwiches, cake fruit and fruit juice.

Dinner: courgette and lemon soup. Carrot & coriander roulade, basmati and wild rice, avocado salad with balsamic vinegar dressing, organic chocolate mousse, choice of herbal or speciality teas, decaffeinated and regular filter coffee.

Opening Times

Year round.

Prices

D+B&B from £28 per person per night.

Public Transport Details

Catch the ferry from Oban to Mull, drive or take the bus to Fionnphort and then by passenger ferry to Iona.

Facilities

J, NS, SD, CH, TC, VP, VR, V, A, E

19. ARGYLL HOTEL

Isle of Iona
Argyll
Tel: 01681 700334
Fax: 01681 700510

Friendly seashore hotel, cosy lounges with open fires, spacious dining room with family portraits, plant-filled sun lounge, cottagey bedrooms with electric blankets and period furniture.

Contact Name

Fiona Menzies

Sample Menus

Breakfast: Breakfast buffet including muesli, our yoghurt etc. plus porridge and choice of cooked breakfasts.

Dinner: Carrot & coriander roulade, mushroom piroshki with sour cream and apple sauce.Petite pots au chocolate/cheese board.

Opening Times

Easter to October

Prices

D+B&B £54–£60 per person

Public Transport Details

Take ferry from Oban to Craigmure on Mull

Bus/car across Mull. Ferry from Fionnphort to Iona. We are 200 yards from Iona jetty.

Facilities

M, F, SR, NR, SD, ES, WHB, TC,
L (restricted), VR, P, C,
V (if requested in advance), E

Among the northern foothills of the Grampians by the River Spey lies 'The Malt Whisky Trail'. If you like whisky – and even if you don't – you can visit eight distilleries as you travel around this beautiful area in the east corner of Scotland. This ancient landscape has seen turbulent times. It is world-famous castle country – there are seventy of them! 25% of all the standing stones in Britain are also to be found in this area. Scotland's ski slopes are here, as well as surfing, yachting and hill-walking opportunities.

Aberdeen is Scotland's 'big country' world famous seascapes, rivers and heatherclad hills and mountains are everywhere you look. Aberdeen is also famous for its festivals and fairs which add to the atmosphere of its unique culture where the local dialect of 'Doric' can still be heard. Aberdeen is described as 'the flower of Scotland' and a 'shining city'. It is also home to Europe's biggest indoor garden –'The Duthie Park'.

With Balmoral Castle the holiday place of the 'Royals' since Queen Victoria, Ballater is recognisable by the quantity of 'by appointment' signs on the shop doors.

The Findhorn Foundation has to be seen to be believed, triple home of the wondeful Eileen Caddy, eternal sunshine, and my publisher! Nearby Forres is a floral town where in the summer you can see the most fabulous animals made from flowers and things. It is also the only place I know where you can buy 'Veggie' shoes while having a meal!

Banff and Buchan was once an area of open moorland. In the late 18th century and early 19th century, agricultural improvements transformed this area and most of the inland villages date from this period.

The Cairngorm Mountains, Satrosphere, Duthie Park Winter Gardens, Archaelink, The Findhorn Foundation, Braemar Gathering.

Aberdeen and Grampian Tourist Board	Vegan Contact
Migvie House	George Rodger.
North Silver Street	17 Howburn Place,
Aberdeen	Aberdeen
AB10 1RJ	01224 573034

38

Health Food Shops

• **Balance.**
High Street, Fochaber
01343 821443

• **Kimbro Health Foods**
40 South Street, Elgin
01343 549318

• **Phoenix Community Stores**
The Park, Findhorn,
01309 690110

• **Village Store**
Newton Dee, Bieldside,
Aberdeen
01224 868609

IONA COTTAGE

Non-smoking, Vegetarian Dinner, Bed & Breakfast on the peaceful and beautiful Island of Iona. Come and enjoy fresh air, home cooking and an open fire.

Hester and Ewan, Iona Cottage, Isle of Iona Argyll PA76 6SJ
Telephone 01681 700579

20. INVERDEEN HOUSE B & B

11 Bridge Square, Ballater Royal Deeside AB35 5QJ
Tel: 013397 55759

You'll find a warm reception in a beautiful listed building circa 1820 with period antiques.

Great breakfasts and excellent beds (2 are King size!). Superb B & B.

We speak English, French, German and Polish.

Very near River Dee, a splendid Highland scenery. Hillwalking, cycling, pony trekking, archery and more nearby.

Positively no smoking. Brochure on request.

Contact

Sandy Munroe

Sample Menus

Inverdeen House offers four scrumptious breakfasts: Canadian, Scottish vegetarian, and by arrangement, vegan.

Our recipes are all 'from scratch'. We treat our guest to home-made muffins with home made jam.

The Canadian breakfast features pancakes with Maple syrup.

Vegans may have packed lunches and may take their evening meal with us "en famille" by arrangement.

We offer knowledgeable special dietary meals with personal interest and integrity.

Opening Times

All year (closed noon to 4pm daily)

Prices

£15–£18 per person per night

Facilities

M, F, NS, SD, CH, TC, VR, C, A, V, E

✴ *5% discount to readers of this guide*

21. GORDON ARMS HOTEL

Kincardine O' Neil
Royal Deeside
Aberdeenshire
AB34 5AA
Tel: 013398 84236
Fax: 013398 84401

Small family run hotel in oldest village on Royal Deeside. Formerly a Victorian coaching inn, the hotel has comfortable en suite rooms with central heating, tea making facilities and colour television. Centrally positioned for touring and for all the local attractions.Lunches, afternoon teas, high teas, bar suppers, dinners. Vegetarian menu always available. Real ales and organic wines

Contact

Bryn Wayte

Sample Menus

Lunch: Garlic mushrooms, chilled fruit juice Vegetarian chilli con carne Vegetarian Lasagne, Omelettes, Ploughman's lunch, vegetarian burger, Baked potatoes - plain, cheese, baked beans, cheese & pineapple

Bar Supper: Vegetarian chilli con carne Vegetarian lasagne, cheese salad, vegetarian burger, samosas, deep fried mushrooms, citrus cocktail, brie on a branch, garlic bread.

Opening Times

11.30am–11pm

Directions

On main A93 Aberdeen–Braemar Road.

Facilities

M, F, NR, DA, SD, CH, WHB, TC, L, VR, P, C, E

22. ARCHAEOLINK

Berryhill
Oyne
Insch
Aberdeenshire
AB52 6QT
Tel: 01467 620981
Fax: 01467 620981

Archaeolink, pre-history park, opening Spring 1997. Interactive exhibition of world class standard to bring alive the story of the pre historic people of the North east.

We offer vegetarian/vegan food.

The building is a tribute to sustainability having been built without a central heating system, but insulate by being covered in earth - truly a 'Green building'!

Contact

Karen Smith

Opening Times

All year

Prices

£3.90 adult/£2.35 child, concessions

Public Transport Details

Nearest train station: Insch (4 miles)

See Map on Page 49

23. CASTLE OF PARK

Cornhill
Banffshire
AB4 2AX
Tel: 01466 751 667
Fax : 01466 751 667

16th Century Castle in peaceful setting near Banffshire coast. Relaxed friendly atmosphere with choice of accommodation from private four poster suites to small groups. Restaurant open to all. Art Gallery also offers range of painting holidays.

Contact

Meryl Duncan

Sample Menus

Breakfast: usual selection & veggie sausages; mushroom and cheese baked butteries; Eggy bread with herb baked tomatoes.

Dinner: Potato and nettle pancakes with creamed garlic mushrooms. Nut pate set in a cabbage tarte with a rich tomato and red wine sauce. Raspberry & white chocolate cranachan.

Opening Times

12–3pm & 7–9pm (check winter opening.)

Prices

Dinner – 3 course average £12
also special D+B&B breaks.

Public Transport Details

Bus from Buckie, Banff or Aberdeen. Train (12 miles) Huntly then taxi (lift may be arranged – please phone).

Facilities:

M, F, SR, NR, DA, DF, SD, CH, TC, L, VP, VA, P, C, V

24. NEPTUNE GUEST HOUSE

22/24 Tolboth Street
Forres
IV36 0PH
Tel: 01309 674387
Fax: 01309 674387

Neptune House is a 17th century modernised Scottish Townhouse offering every modern convenience whilst retaining its traditional character and charm. It is situated in a quiet location just off Forres High Street, ideally placed for all local amenities. We also boast our own fully licensed vegetarian/vegan restaurant – *Verdant* – which offers a range of snacks and meals throughout the day.

Contact

John & Louise Cousens

Sample Menus

Breakfast: Free range eggs, vegetarian sausages, tomatoes, mushrooms, fruit juice, yoghurt, fresh fruit.

Lunch: Vegetarian or vegan soups, variety of sandwiches, baked potatoes, home-made cakes, biscuits & desserts.

Dinner: Tofu & vegetable kebabs, mushroom & chestnut bake, carrot & cashew savoury bake, Lentil pie etc. etc.

Snacks: Garlic Nan bread with humus, deep fried brie wedges, various pies & pastries home-made cakes biscuits.

Opening Times

Guest house open all year. Restaurant 9am–5pm Evenings 5pm–9pm

Prices

£15.50–£18.50 per person per night.

Facilities

J, SR, NR, SD, CH, ES, TC, L , VP, VA, P, C, V, A, E

J

25. HEALTH WORKS

5 Bank Lane
Forres
IV36 0NO
Tel: 01309 676691
Fax: 01309 674911

A medically supervised health and wellness programme to support you to make healthy choices in your life – in diet, life style, preventative health care or rehabilitation as well as in situations of chronic illness.

Contact:

Dr C. J. Featherstone

Opening Times

9.30–12.30am & 2.30–5.40pm
Consultations by appointment.

26. MINTON HOUSE

Findhorn
Forres
Moray
IV36 0YY
Tel: 01309 690819
Fax: 01309 691583

Minton House is a magnificent pink mansion on the shore of Findhorn Bay. When you walk in you immediately feel the space. On entering the meditation room, peace surrounds you. Our main purpose is to provide an environment which exerts its healing influence on our guests. Minton is a retreat centre honouring all the main spiritual traditions, situated next to the Findhorn Foundation in an area well-known for its natural beauty and wildlife. Activities available include massage, yoga, Taize singing and dance, and our year round programme of workshops and retreats.

Sample Menus

Breakfast: buffet of wholefood meuslis, cereals, fresh baked bread from the Findhorn bakery fresh fruit and fruit salad of apricots, figs, prunes etc.

Lunch by arrangement;soup and salads

Dinner by arrangement: 2 course, home cooking of wholesome vegetarian cuisine.

Opening Times

Closed January

Prices

B&B £15–£27; Lunch £3.50; Dinner £6

Public Transport Details

Planes, trains or buses to Inverness or Aberdeen. Train, bus or taxi to Forres. Taxi to Minton.

Facilities

F, NS, NR (weekends only), DA, SD, CH, TC, VP, VR, C, V, E

Healthy Choices Made Easy

Healthy Holidays

A medically supervised health and wellness programme to support you to make healthy choices in your life - in diet, life style, preventative health care and rehabilitation as well as in chronic illness.

Health Works

FORRES CENTRE FOR HOLISTIC HEALTH CARE
5 Bank Lane, Forres,
Morayshire IV36 ONU

For further information please contact us on
Tel: 01309-676691
Mon-Fri 9.30-12.30, and 2.30-5.30pm
or on
Fax: 01309-674911

27. CAFE HELIOS

Findhorn Foundation
The Park
Findhorn
Forres
IV36 OTZ
Tel: 01309 691900
Fax: 01309 691301

Café Helios is in The Park, seat of the Findhorn Foundation, an international spiritual community. Specialising in quality cross-cultural vegetarian café cuisine, serving Italian and American coffee, French cakes and pastries, cold drinks, snacks and freshly prepared lunches, which include quiche, pizza, savoury croissants, soup, filled baguettes, etc. Outdoor patio and a peaceful atmosphere surrounded by beautiful gardens.

Limited Vegan menu.

Opening Times

Monday 12.30–5pm

Tuesday–Saturday 10am–5pm

Sunday 12–5pm

Prices

Various – Savoury croissants £1.75, Cakes £1.65, cappuccino 80p, tea 50p, coffee 55p

28. HELOISE SHEWAN

72 Findhorn
Forres
Moray
IV36 OYF
Tel: 01309 690495

Fisherman style cottage well kept and artistically decorated, well maintained, with wood burning stove (artist and architect's daughter!) in peaceful north-eastern coastal location, with milder climate due to Gulf stream, on doorstep of the famous Findhorn Foundation Spiritual Community.

Contact

Heloise Shewan

Sample Menus

Breakfast: Melon (Gala) with strawberries, kiwis, with or without brown sugar, croissants, various selections of organic spreads, chocolate croissants, mushroom cooked in butter with melted cheese in omelette, cheese board with organic bread home-baked at Phoenix bakery, Findhorn Foundation.

Opening Times

January–December

Prices

£15 double/twin 2 in room.

£17.50 double twin 1 in room.

Facilities

M, F, SD, TC, VA, P, C, E,
V (cheese on request)

The Highlands and Skye now make up the biggest Scottish Tourist Board area, but like most other areas suffer from the problem that you cannnot lump together so many places and expect to describe them in a few sentences. I'll give it a go anyway...

Fort William & Lochaber

In Fort William and Lochaber, you will find Britain's highest mountain, deepest loch, a sub-tropical garden and a snowed-capped summit. You will also find busy towns, peaceful villages and unspoilt beaches. Wildlife observers should look out for deer, otters, badgers, wildcats and pinemartins.

Aviemore & the Spey Valley

Badenoch and Strathspey is the place for every-one whether young or old, on your own or with a party, in search of peace and quiet or excitement. Walkers of all levels will find 'their hill' here and hopefully on the way up see some wildlife or birds of prey such as osprey or eagles.There is also skiing in winter, and water sports in summer on Loch Morlisct.

Inverness

Inverness, capital of the Highlands, has all the city attractions of bars, restaurants and plenty to do. It has a theatre, a cinema, a bowling alley and an ice skating rink. However, in just a few minutes you can be in the wilds of the Highlands or on the trail of Scotland's most famous inhabitant – yes, Nessie is here and even the most sceptical of you will enjoy the legend and I bet you find yourself having just a little look! A little further on is beautiful Urquhart Castle, the venue in 1996 for another battle – this one was not fought against the English, it was fought against the developers who wanted to change this site beyond recognition. As you stand and behold this awesome monument you will be relieved that this last battle has been won by the locals.

Caithness & Sutherland
with help from Lesley Black, Port Na Con Guest House

The Norse influence to this eastern-most tip of Scotland is well evident: Viking names are predominant. Here you will discover what 'getting away from it all' holidays are all about. John O' Groats is here and surfers can ride the waves at nearby Pentland Firth

Loch Eribol was famous during the World War II as the place where the Murmansk Convoy ships congregated before sailing northeast to Russia; the names of the ships can be seen on the hillside above the village of Laid. Apparently the sailors, having nothing better to do, were sent up the hill to pick out the name of their own ship and white paint the stones depicting the other ships' names, and because they always got caught here in bad weather the loch became known as 'Loch Orrible' or 'Terrible Eriboll'. We have had several ex-sailors return and stay and each one has a different tale to tell.

Durness is a convenient stop off for Munro 'Baggers' and is centrally sited for Ben Hope and Foinhaven – and yes, I know that it is not officially a Munro, but a report a few years ago suggested that it should be since now that it has been re-measured by satellite, it is in excess of 3000 feet. Obviously, it has either grown or early tape measures did not stretch far enough!

Both Cape Wrath and Faraid Head are famous for the nesting puffins in May–June and there are several seal colonies there and in Eribol. We have fantastic beaches – beautiful golden sands, a nine hole golf course, boat trips, Smoo caves and a craft village.

Ross & Cromarty

Once over the Kessock Bridge, you are in 'Ross and Cromarty' which comprises Easter Ross, Wester Ross and The Black Isle. Described as 'the last great wilderness', it is home to the most diverse selection of wildlife including the golden eagle, and one of only two remaining UK colonies of wild dolphins are in the Moray Firth. The Gaelic culture is all around you as is the 'unhurried' Highlands: you will get nothing quickly here, the Spanish word of 'mañana' meaning tomorrow has a not-so-rushed Gaelic equivalent of **uaireigin,** meaning simply 'sometime–anytime, just not today'.

There are distilleries, hills , unspoilt beaches, diverse attractions like the 'Achiltibuie Hydroponichum' and a waterfall higher than Niagara. As many talented and artistic incomers have made the North West Highlands their home, the place is heaving with art and craft studios.

The roads up here are something else and certainly not for the faint-hearted, in particular the road from Torridon to Diabaig is scarier than any rollercoaster I've ever been on (Disney, eat your heart out).

Skye

So much has been written about Skye that I can't add anything new. It's here, it's beautiful, and it now has a bridge instead of a ferry (boo hoo). For those of you who prefer to go over the sea to Skye, you can reach it by ferry via Malaig.

Highlands of Scotland Tourist Board
Tourist Information Centre
Aviemore
Inverness-shire
PH22 1PP
Tel: 0990 143070
Fax: 01479 811063

Vegan Contacts
Jackie Redding. Taigh Na Mara,
Lochbroom, Nr. Ullapool. IV23 2SE.
01854 655282
Maralyn Shine. Inverness Veggies,
PO Box 1, Drumnadrochit, Highlands
01456 450496

Health Food Shops

• **The Fruit & Nut Place**
Dunvegan, Isle of Skye
01470 521480

• **Health Food Shop**
5 Princes Street, Thurso
01847 893561

• **The Health Shop**
20 Baron Taylor Street, Inverness
01463 233104

• **Jackson's Wholefoods**
Park Lane, Portree, Skye
01478 613326

• **Epicurus**
5 Leopold Street, Nairn
01167 452874

• **The Wee Health Shop**
3,Market Hall, Inverness
01463 710255

The Gordon Arms Hotel

Kincardine O'Neil • Royal Deeside

A small family run hotel in oldest village on
Royal Deeside. Formerly a Victorian
coaching inn, the hotel has comfortable en
suite rooms with central heating, tea making
facilities and colour television. Centrally
positioned for touring and for all the local
attractions.Lunches, afternoon teas, high
teas, bar suppers, dinners.

Vegetarian menu always available.

Real ales and organic wines

On the main A93 Aberdeen–Braemar Road
Tel. 013398 84236 • Fax. 013398 84401

29. CRAIGELLACHIE HOUSE

Main Street
Newtonmore
Inverness-shire
PH20 1DA
Tel.: 01540 673360

Bed and Breakfast

Contact

Kathryn Main

Sample Menus

Breakfast: porridge made with organic oats, yoghurt, fresh and dried fruits, mushrooms and tomato on toast, fruit filled pancakes, fruit and herb tea, home-made jams, our own eggs when the hens are laying.

Opening Times

All year except Christmas

Prices

£15–£20

Public Transport Details

Buses and trains stop in Newtonmore. Inverness airport 50 miles.

Facilities

**M, F, NS, SD, CH, TC, VA,
P (by arrangement), C, V, A, E**

30. SONNHALDE GUEST HOUSE

East Terrace
Kingussie
Inverness-shire
PH21 1JS
Tel.: 01540 661266
Fax: 01540 661266

Warm, friendly modernised Victorian villa with views overlooking Cairngorm mountains.

Contact

Mr & Mrs Jones

Sample Menus

Selection of cereals, Greek yoghurt, fruit compote, rolls, scones, traditional cooked breakfast (ie. eggs, tomatoes mushrooms etc.)

Home-made soup, cheese spinach pie with fresh vegetables. Spiced apple & honey mousse.

Opening Time

January–October

Prices

B&B from £17.50. Dinner from £9

Public Transport Details

Five minutes walk from train or bus. From High Street run left at traffic lights, 1st right, we are 3rd house on left.

Facilities

**M, F, SR, SD, CH, WHB, TC, VR,
P (by arrangement), C, V, E**

31. GLEN FESHIE HOSTEL

Balchroick, Kincraig
Inverness-shire PH21 1NH
Tel. 01540 651323

Set in beautiful Glen Feshie with immediate access to the Cairngorm National Nature Reserve we are deally placed for walking, climbing, and cycling, and in winter a perfect base for cross country skiing. 3 bunk rooms each with four beds, one with two beds and one single room. Fully equiped kitchen for self catering. All meals can be provided. Mountain bike hire, Nordic skiing equipment hire and ski instruction.

Sample Menus

Breakfast: Porridge, home-made bread, fresh juice, yoghurt dried & fresh fruit, mushrooms on toast, free range eggs

Dinner: Home-made soups. Stuffed mushrooms, cauliflower mustard soufflé, aubergine ragout, wild mushroom strudel with wine sauce, vegetable gadogado, all served with fresh vegetables and herbs form garden when available. Lemon pavlova individual orange and walnut puddings with fudge sauce.

Opening Times

All year

Prices

£7 (includes porridge). £2.50 extra for cooked breakfast. Evening meal £5–£8. Packed lunch £2.50

Public Transport Details

Train or bus to Kingussie or Aviemore, where you can get picked up from. GR849009 from Kingussie take B9151 to Kincraig turn right at Kincraig, down unclassified road for 2km turn left onto the B970 towards Feshiebridge. After crossing the river Feshie in 1.5km turn right onto a road signposted hostel 2 miles.

Facilities

F, NS, SD, WHB, VP, VA, P, C, V, E

32. AVINGORMACK GUEST HOUSE

Boat of Garten
Inverness-shire
PH24 3BT
Tel: 01479 831614

Country guest house situated on a wooded hill with breathtaking views of the Cairngorm mountains. Our emphasis is on quality imaginitive vegetarian cuisine. Winner of the Vegetarian Menu of the Year Highly Commended Award 1994, presented by the Association of Vegetarian Caterers with Rose Elliot. Skiiing available from £11 per day.

Contact

Jan Ferguson

Sample Menus

Breakfast: Spiced fruit compote, home made hot muffins and scones, sweet corn fritters, mushroom crepes, vegetarian cooked breakfast, fresh coffee, choice of teas. Dinner: Home made soups hot savoury souffles baked goats cheese served on a bed of leaves with walnut dressing, courgette roulade with tomato and garlic filling, black eyed bean and vegetable casserole with a polenta crust, wild mushroom strudel with red wine sauce, steamed chocolate and walnut pudding, tropical fruit platter with lychee sorbet, heather honey and whiskey ice cream, scottish vegetarian cheeses with oat cakes, fresh brewed coffee and mints

Opening Times

December 27th–November 1st

Prices

B&B from £19.50. 4-course dinner £14

Facilities

M, F, NS, SD, CH, WHB, TC, VP, VR, C, V, E

THE CEILIDH PLACE

14 West Argyle Stree, Ullapool, Wester Ross IV26 2TY

Tel 01854 612103 Fax 01854 612886

HOTEL, COFFEE SHOP, RESTAURANT, BARS, BUNK HOUSE,

CONCERTS, CEILIDHS, EXHIBITIONS

write or call for a copy of our menu, programme of events & brochure

JOHN MACLEAN
BAKER & GENERAL MERCHANT
Shore Street, Ulllapool, Wester Ross
Tel 01854 612488 Fax 01854 612488

BAKERY, CAFE, PURVEYOR OF FINE WINES, TEAS & WHOLEFOODS, GIFTS, HOUSEHOLD WARES, DRAPERY, BOOTS &SHOES

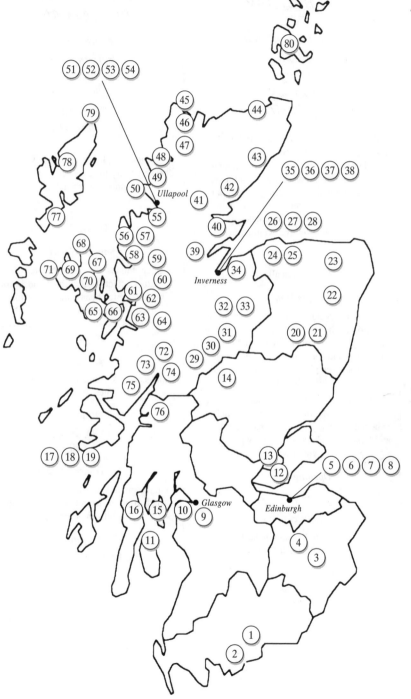

49

51 52 53 54

79

78

45
46
47
48
49
50
Ullapool
55

44

43

35 36 37 38

42
41
40
39

26 27 28

24 25

23

22

34
Inverness

56 57
58 59
60
61 62
63 64
65 66

68
67
70
71 69

77

32 33

31
30
29
72
73 74
75
76

14

20 21

13
12

5 6 7 8

17 18 19

16 15 10
9
Glasgow

Edinburgh

11

4
3

1
2

33. SHALIMAR

16 Woodside Avenue
Grantown on Spey
Moray
PH26 3JR
Tel.: 01479 873204

Built at the turn of the Century and in close proximity to the River Spey and beautiful woodland walks, this comfortable, homely, no smoking guest house offers you the best in home cooking and baking. Children (and pets) are made most welcome in this family home and special rates apply. Booking is essential for evening meals.

Contact

Lynne Metcalfe

Sample Menus

Breakfast: Vegetarian sausages, tomatoes, mushrooms, home-made baked beans, free range eggs, home-made breads and cereals yoghurts and fruit salads. Packed lunch: includes home pies, quiches, breads and home baking.

Dinner: Soups & home-made breads always available, Indian vegetarian cuisine a speciality, plenty of pizzas, pastas, salads, and fresh vegetables, all lovingly prepared. Bring your own wine.

Opening Times

All year

Prices

B&B £15–£16. Evening meal £9.50. Packed Lunch £3.50

Facilities

M, NS, NR, SD, CH, WHB, TC, VR, P, C, V, E

34. CULLODEN POTTERY RESTAURANT

The Old Smiddy
Gollanfield
Nr Inverness
IV1 2QT
Tel.: 01667 462749
Fax: 01667 462256

Vegetarian, free range eggs, veggie cheeses, everything we sell is made on the premises fresh daily.

Contact

Denise Park

Sample Menus

Soup, humus and crusty bread, baked potatoes selection of fillings, mushroom burgers, spicy bean burgers, nut roast, mushroom & cashew nut crumble, shepherdess pie, served with baked potato, chips or salad.

Opening Times

7 days a week Summer 9.30am–6.30pm / Winter 10am–5pm

Prices

Snack from £1.80. Main courses from £4.50

Public Transport Details

On the main A96 Inverness to Aberdeen road, 10 miles from Inverness / 6 miles from Nairn.

Facilities

F, DA, DF, SD, L, VP, VA, C, V, E

35. OLD DRUMMOND HOUSE

Oak Avenue
Inverness
IV2 4NX
Tel.: 01463 226301

A warm welcome and mouth-watering vegetarian, vegan and traditional Scottish breakfasts await you in the comfort of our tastefully renovated 220 year old house. Situated in a quiet wooded area only five minutes (by car, bus, bike!) from town centre and a pleasant five minute walk from the river and Ness Islands. Tea and coffee making facilities, small play area, bicycle hire.

Contact

Alison & Andy Menzies

Sample Menu

Breakfast: Spicy fruit compote. Seasonal fresh fruits and juices, cereals, dairy or Soya yoghurts and cheeses, free range eggs, mushrooms, tomatoes, potato rosti veggie-burgers, honey, preserves, herb teas and cafetiere coffees.

Opening Times

January–December

Prices

B&B from £15 (Reductions for children and longer stays)

Public Transport Details

Five minutes walk to two main bus routes. (regular service)

Facilities

M, F, SD, CH, WHB, TC, VA, C, V, E

36. ABB COTTAGE

11 Douglas Row
Inverness
IV1 1RE
Tel.: 01463 233486

Listed building, central, riverside, terraced cottage in quiet one way street. Old fashioned B & B values, evening snacks, in sitting-room. Books, puzzles, games available for guests' use.

Contact

Miss Storrar

Sample Menus

Breakfast: Juices, cereals, grilled tomatoes, cheese, mushroom pate, mushrooms, tomatoes on toast, omelettes. Teas, coffee, decaffeinated and herb teas.

Dinner: Stir fries, bulghar wheat and vegetarian curries, herb egg pate, nut crunch cream.

Opening Times

March–December

Prices

B&B from £14 per person per night in twin room. D+ B&B from £22

Public Transport Details

Walking distance of bus & rail stations.

Facilities

M, F, NS, DA, DF, SD, CH, WHB, VR, C (over 12), V, E

See Map on Page 49

37. HIGHLAND WHOLEFOODS

Wholesale Cash & Carry
& Delivery Service
Unit 6B
13 Harbour Road
Inverness
IV1 1SY
Tel.: 01463 712393
Fax: 01463 715586
E-mail:
hihoco@enterprise.net

We are a workers' co-operative and endeavour to run our business in a socially responsible way:
- We only sell vegetarian or vegan products.
- Whenever possible we buy from other socially responsible organisations and from local suppliers
- We are committed to supplying high quality products back up by a friendly and reliable service.

You can choose from over 4000 lines in our Inverness Cash & Carry. Alternatively, we operate a regular free delivery service throughout the Highlands.

We actively promote an extensive range of organic (including fresh fruit & vegetable "fair traded", and environmentally aware products.

Phone us today and ask for a price list and a copy of the latest edition of our newsletter "The Digest".

38. THE RIVER CAFÉ AND RESTAURANT

10 Bank Street
Inverness
IV1 1QY
Tel. 01463 714884

Café and restaurant beside River Ness serving fresh home cooked food, coffee, home baking etc. in pleasant relaxed atmosphere.

Contact
Anthony Walker

Sample Menus
Mushroom & almond casserole served with mixed salads or potatoes and vegetables, aubergine and sweet potato bake.

Opening Times
Summer 10am–10pm. Winter 10am–8.30pm. Closed Sundays.

Prices
Lunch main course from £4. Dinner main course from £5.25

Public Transport Details
Near Inverness town centre by Greig Street footbridge.

Facilities
M, F, NS, DA, SD, CH, L, VA, C, V, E

39. STATION TEA ROOM AND CRAFT SHOP

Station Square
Dingwall
Ross-shire
IV15 9JD
Tel. 01349 865 894

Family run tea room and shop in renovated waiting rooms at Dingwall Railway Station. Home-made vegetarian soup our speciality.

Contact

Chris & Anne Monckton

Sample Menus

Light meals available all day, freshly baked wholemeal rolls, scones, selection of toasted sandwiches, baked potatoes. Speciality teas and fresh coffee.

Opening Times

10am–4pm (winter) / 10am–5pm (summer)

Prices

Home baking from 70p. Soup £1.30. Filled rolls from £1

Facilities

NS, DA, DF, CH, VP, C, E

40. MANSEFIELD HOUSE HOTEL

Scotsburn Road
Tain
Ross-shire
IV19 1PR
Tel.: 01862 892052
Fax: 01862 892260

Elegant country house hotel, perfectly situated for touring the Highlands, all parts of which can be reached in a series of one day driving tours. STB 4 Crown Highly Commended, AA/RAC 3 stars, Taste of Scotland.

Contact

Norman Lauritsen

Sample Menus

Both our bar and a la carte restaurant menus contain a good selection of vegetarian dishes. We are happy to arrange full vegetarian menus by prior arrangement. Vegetarian evenings are held periodically. Wide selection of malt whiskies and real ales.

Facilities

M, F, NR, DA, SD, CH, ES, TC, L, VR, C

See Map on Page 49

41. INVERCASSLEY COTTAGE

Rosehall by Lairg
Sutherland
IV27 4BD
Tel.: 01549 441 288

Set in a large wooded garden, Invercassley cottage is an interesting blend of old and new. The sun lounge/dining room overlooks Strathoykel and is ideally placed for walking, climbing and cycling being within an hours drive from N, W &E coasts. Children are very welcome and canoes and mountain bikes may be available for hire. Campers welcome.

Contact
Pam Menzies

Sample Menus
Good healthy home cooking.

Breakfast: Home-made bread, jams, marmalade, selection of teas or coffee, yoghurt, fruit cooked breakfast including mushrooms courgettes, eggs tomatoes.

Dinner: Two course with interesting soup or sweets made from garden fruits.Courgette bake, red dragon pie, bean casseroles stir fries, using high quality ingredients.

Opening Times
All year

Prices
B&B £14. Evening meal £6. Reductions for children

Public Transport Details
Train to Lairg – can be met at Station.
Bus once a day Lairg – Lochinver

Facilities
M, F, CH, WHB, TC, VR, C, E

42. STATION HOUSE

Rogart
Sutherland
IV28 3XA
Tel.: 01408 641343

Twin bedded, en suite room in former waiting room on working station.

Contact
Kate Roach

Sample Menus
Breakfast: porridge, cereals, free range eggs, veggie-sausage, mushrooms, baked beans, tomato home-made bread, orange juice, tea coffee, fruit tea.

Dinner: hazelnut & vegetarian loaf, lentil moussaka, lentil & mushroom gratin. Broccoli & cheese flan. Organic home-grown vegetables when possible, chocolate mousse, lemon flan.

Opening Times
All year

Prices
£13 per person. £15 single person occupancy. Evening meal by arrangement £6

Public Transport Details
We are a working station.

Facilities
NS, DA, DF, CH, ES, TC, VP, VR, C, V, A, E

Key to Facilities is on Page 13

43. FIR BRAE CROFT HOUSE

189 Marrel Helmsdale
Sutherland K8 6HU
Tel.: 01431 821223

Modernised croft house in quiet crofting township approximately 2 miles from Helmsdale. Accommodation available – 1 twin, 1 family room with double bed & 2 single beds (sleeps 4), 1 single room. Smoking not encouraged. Fully vegetarian meals available – vegan by prior arrangement.

Contact

Barbara Grainger

Sample Menus

Breakfast: Fresh fruit and/or fruit juice, muesli, porridge, and/or hot meal with or without free range eggs etc.

Dinner: nut loafs, pilaffs, various vegetarian bakes, pastas, salads, cakes, puddings and compotes.

Opening Times

March–November

Prices

B&B £13.50 per person. Dinner £4–£6.50

Public Transport Details:

Railway station 1 mile.

Bus in village – collection from bus stop or station may be arranged.

Facilities

M, F, NS, SD, CH (partial), TC, VR, P, C, V, E

44. CREAG-NA-MARA

East Mey
By Thurso
Caithness
KW14 8XL
Tel.: 01847 851713

Licensed restaurant with accommodation which is open to non residents and also caters for special diets. Our conservatory restaurant is beautifully situated with views of The Orkneys and Dunnet Head and close to the Castle of Mey. Shooting and fishing are available.

We cater for vegetarian and special diets and have some facilities for the disabled. There is no increase for lone travellers who are most welcome, as are children and pets. 2 rooms en suite , 2 rooms with shared facilities.

Contact

Glenys & Norman Kimber

Sample Menus

Home-made soups – pumpkin & orange, French mushroom, cauliflower and vegetable. Vegetarian meals using our own recipes and fresh vegetables, home-made desserts, cheese & biscuits and fresh fruit.

Prices

B&B from £16 per person. D+B&B from £26

Facilities

NR, DF, SD, CH, ES, P, C

45. CHORAIDH CROFT

94 Laid Loch Eribollside
By Altnaharra
Lairg
Sutherland
Tel: 01971 511235

Tearoom/restaurant on shore of beautiful Loch Eriboll. Spectacular views. Farm park adjacent. B&B in house

Contact

Lesley Smith

Sample Menus

Breakfast: muesli, fresh fruit compote, free range eggs, yoghurt.

Snacks/lunch: home-made soups, quiche, baked potatoes, wholemeal sandwiches, salads.

Dinner: vegetables en croute, walnut & cashew nut roast, stir fry, savoury pasta & pancakes, carrot cake, fresh fruit salad, pineapple meringue pudding.

Opening Times

9.30am–8.30pm

Prices

B&B from £14. Dinner £8 (varies).
Lunch £3

Facilities

M, F, NS, NR, DA, CH, TC, VR, C, A, T, SD & V (by prior arrangement)

46. PORT NA CON HOUSE

Loch Eriboll
By Altnahara
Lairg
Sutherland
IV27 4UN
Tel.: 01971 511 367
Fax: 01971 511 367

Built approx. 200 years ago, Port-Na-Con House is sited on the West shore of Loch Eriboll, 7 miles east of Durness. We have a reputation for good food in comfortable and tranquil surroundings, with homely and personal service.

Contact

Lesley Black

Sample Menus

Home-made soup, vegetables, carrot & cottage cheese parcels, Mange tout stir fried with garlic and ginger, Fruity brandy snaps.

Opening Times

Mid-March to Mid-October

Prices

£16.50–£18.50 per person B&B. Single supplement £6 per person June/July/August
Dinner £11

Public Transport Details

Situated just off A838 7 miles east of Durness, on shore of Loch Eriboll, Post bus from Lairg 9am. Return 11.30am Monday to Saturday.

Facilities

M, F, NS, SD, CH, WHB, TC, L, P, C, V, E NR (8.30pm by prior arrangement)

47. THE COFFEE SHOP

Balnakiel Craft Village
Durness
By Lairg
Sutherland
IV27 4PT
Tel.: 01206 298824

Friendly, informal occasionally chaotic, vegetarian coffee shop in the centre of a working craft village. We serve soup and wholesome goodies to the intrepid traveller and take-away cakes And filled rolls to picnickers.

Contact

Brenda Gamlin

Sample Menus

Light meals and filling soup available all day. Freshly baked rolls and cakes; home-made jam, pancakes-sweet and savoury, filter and decaffeinated coffee, fruit & herb teas.

Opening Times

10am–6pm late May to end of August. (Closed Sundays in June & early July)

Prices

Snacks from £1.50

Public Transport Details

From Inverness: train to Lairg, postbus to Durness or summer bus Inverness-Durness. Balnakeil is 3/4 mile west of Durness village centre.

Facilities

J, NS, DA, DF, SD, WHB, VA, C, V, E

48. SOLUS NA MARA

Clashmore
Lochinver
Stoer
IV27 4JQ
Tel: 01571 855396

Warm, welcoming bright croft house 2 letting bedrooms, 1 family, 1 twin room.

Contact

Maureen Shannon

Sample Menus

Breakfast: Fruit, cereal, scrambled eggs, mushrooms & potato scones.

Dinner: Courgette & spinach soup, Leek & Oat flan and various salads, selection of home-made ice cream.

Opening Times

All year – except Christmas

Prices

B & B from £16. Dinner £10

Public Transport Details

Train to Inverness. Bus to Ullapool. Possible collection from Ullapool £10

Facilities

F, NS, SD, CH, ES, TC, VP, P, C, V, E
Person-centred counselling by prior arrangements.

See Map on Page 49

49. ACHINS COFFEE SHOP

Inverkirkaig
Lochinver
Sutherland
Tel.: 01571 844 262
Fax: 01571 844 262

Small coffee shop adjacent to bookshop
with seating for 28. Picture gallery also of
some local artists.

Contact

A. J. Dickson

Sample Menus

There is always a soup of the day,
lunchtime dishes will include nut roast,
quiche, baked potatoes, range of home
baking always available. Menu will vary
through the season according to demand.

Opening Times

10am–5pm all week Easter to October

Facilities

NS, DA, DF, C

50. HYDROPONICUM

Achiltibuie
Nr. Ullapool
IV26 2YG
Tel. 01854 622 202
Fax 01854 622 201

Garden of the Future

Contact

Terry Grimshaw

Opening Times

April–September 10am–6pm

Prices

£3.50 adult. 3.00 Concession. £2.00 child
free under 5 years

Facilities

V, E

The Hydroponicum
Achiltibuie

Hourly guided tours of the unique
indoor garden without soil. Relax in
the pleasant atmosphere of the
Lilypond Café & enjoy our own
fresh produce, home cooked meals
and light snacks.

51a. THE CEILIDH PLACE

West Argyle Street
Ullapool
IV26 2TY
Tel.: 01854 612103
Fax: 01854 612886

Internationally famous unique Hotel, Bunkhouse, Coffee shop, Restaurant, Bookshop, Bars. Open all year – write for programme of events, concerts & ceilidhs.

Facilities

M, F, NR, WHB, TC, L, VP, VA, P, C, V, E

51b JOHN MACLEANS GENERAL STORE

Shore street,
Ullapool
Tel: 01854 612488.

Owned by the same people who are behind The Ceilidh Place this is a Bakers, Cáfé, Health food and General store right on the Ullapool seafront. Excellent wholesome home baked bread, potato scones, donuts and cakes without the chemicals. Organic beers and wines and a treasure trove of other goodies from fresh ginger,Herb teas or capers to aromatherapy, clothes and shoes.

Upstairs is the cafe where they do a mean veggie burger and the chips are some of the best you'll get anywhere.From the window seats you can watch the fishing boats coming and going or keep an eye out for the Stornaway ferry.

Opening Times

All year – 7 days a week in summer.

Facilities

SD, E, V

52. PENNY BROWNE B&B

3 Castle Terrace
Ullapool
Wester Ross
IV26 2XD
Tel.: 01854 612409

Bungalow in peaceful road looking out to sea has pretty rooms and welcoming atmosphere.

Contact

Penny Ross Browne

Sample Menus

Minted melon and strawberries. Porridge, cereals, mixed vegetarian grill, home-made jams, oatcakes, herb or plain tea, cafetiere coffee.

Opening Times

May–September

Prices

£14–£16. Over 2 nights 10% discount.

Public Transport Details

Five minutes walk from bus/ferry terminal.

Facilities

J, NS, DA, CH, WHB, VP, VA, P, C, V, E

53. LADYSMITH GUEST HOUSE

Ladysmith Street
Ullapool
Wester Ross
IV26 2UP
Tel.: 01854 612185

Family run Guest House with licensed dining room open to non-residents.

Contact

Lauri Chiltern

Sample Menus

Full Veggie cooked breakfast. Dnner - garlicky, pepper and pasta, spinach and stilton and mushroom bake, leak and bean pie. Vegan ice cream

Opening Times

All year 6.30pm–9pm

Prices

B&B £13–£22.50
D+B&B £33–£40 per person per night.

Public Transport Details

Bus to Strathpeffer, Dingwall, Inverness.
Ferry to Isle of Lewis, (Stornoway) Not Sundays.

Facilities

M, F, NR, DA, DF, SD, CH, WHB, TC, L, VR, P, C, V, E

* 5% discount to readers of this guide

54. TAIGH NA MARA VEGETARIAN GUESTHOUSE

The Shore, Ardindrean
Lochbroom
Nr Ullapool IV23 2SE
Tel: 01854 655282
Fax:01854 655292

Notorious and grossly over praised home of the authors of "Rainbows & Wellies" (Cookbook of "Scottish Vegan food to sigh for")No road, no smoking, no tarmac carpark, no hanging baskets, no TV, no set time for breakfast, no polite notices, no sense of the rediculous just lots of something you can't quite put your finger on.

Contact

Tony or Jackie

Sample Menus

Breakfast:The works! If you can't see it just ask! Lunch; No one ever had the stamina!
Dinner:Lemon & Coconut Mousse, Baked Onions Stuffed with Haggis, Vegan Pancakes with oyster mushrooms, leeks & pinenuts, Seaweed Roly Poly with Organic Vegetables, Orgasmic Chocolate Vegan Mousse or Vegan Loganberry Blamange Hearts.Vegan Cheese.

Opening Times

All year

Prices

D+B&B £33–£38 per person per night

Public Transport Detail

Bus from Inverness will drop you off 4 miles from the house– lifts can be arranged

Facilities

J, NS, SD,CH, ES, VP, VA, P, C, V, A, E

* 5% discount to readers of this guide

55. SAMADHAN

Scoraig
Dundonnell
By Garve
Wester Ross
IV23 2RE
Tel.: 01854 633 260

Comfortable, isolated, wilderness, abundant wildlife, friendly, relaxed atmosphere communal residents lounge with log fire, spring water on tap, large meditation space, in 2½ acres of organic woodland and organic gardens. Stunning views and walks.

Contact

John Sangster

Sample Menus

Breakfast: help yourself any time (muesli, cereal, porridge, home-made breads etc.)
Lunch: Simple packed lunch/soup etc., on request.
Dinner: Indian, Chinese, Italian traditional (veggie)/jump at the cupboard door.

Opening Times

All year

Prices

D+B&B £26 per person.

Public Transport Details:

Train to Inverness, Wester bus: Monday, Wednesday, Saturday to Badluarach jetty, the wee ferry across little Loch Broom from Badluarach to Samadhan. Alternatively 4 mile walk from road end at Badrallach.

Facilities

J, SD, CH, TC, VP, VR, V, A , E

56. THE MOUNTAIN RESTAURANT & LODGE

Strath Square , Gairloch
Wester Ross IV21 2BX
Tel. 01445 712316

Unique themed restaurant featuring mountaineering, memorabilia, alpine conservatory and Lochside sun terrace. Specialist espresso coffee shop by day, candlelit dinners nightly, with an emphasis on fun and informality, 'laid back' very welcoming atmosphere, Equally unique is the attached 'nature shop'. Accommodation also available. All rooms en suite, most with sea views to Isle of Skye. "4 poster" suite available.

Contact

Andrew Rudge

Sample Menus

Breakfast: homemade muesli with hawaiian nuts, toast or croissants with organic cold pressed honey, fresh scottish strawberries, porridge with fruit toppings, over 60 different teas plus expresso, cappucino and speciality coffees.

Lunch: fresh vegetables and herbs soup, filled croissants, Appalachian apple pie, giant cheese and zucchini muffins, blueberry and ginger scones, veggie quiches.

Dinner: vegetable samosas with yoghurt herb dip, simple spinach lug, Orkney cheese, herb and garlic croissant, misty mountain salad, homemade deserts, 'mountain wines'.

Opening Times

Easter to November and New Year holidays

Prices

B&B from £19.95 per person per night.
Candlelit dinner from £7.95

Facilities

M, F, SR, NR, DA(to restaurant), CH, WHB, TC, L, VP, P, C, V, E

62

57. SAIL GAIRLOCH

Marine Life Centre
Strath Seafront
Gairloch
Ross shire
IV21 2BT
Tel: 01445 712326

Marine Wildlife Cruises. Regular daily sailings. Our visitor centre has photo and video displays of our surveys of local whales, dolphins and porpoise, with even more in 1996 on seabird and seal activity. 1996 had 1029 sightings of the whale family, up a third on 1995. Join one of our cruises, both on 10 metre boats, sailing ketch with 5, or motor with 11 passengers. Licensed and run to "sea watch" code as approved by SNH. Great surroundings too.

Also Seafront self catering cottages

Contact

Ian & Ann Birks

58. RUA REIDH LIGHTHOUSE HOTEL

Melvaig, Gairloch
IV21 2EA
Tel.: 01445 771263
Fax: 01445 771263
email:
ruardieh@netcomuk.co.uk

Hostel offering a wide range of accommodation from self catering hostel room to en suite dinner, B & B.

Contact

Fran Cree

Sample Menus

Breakfast: Cereals, porridge, free range eggs from our own hens, homemade jams, herb teas and fresh coffee.

Evening Meal: Lentil moussaka, hazlenut and vegetable loaf, mushroom gougere, date and apple shortcake, Highland cream, fruit crumble. Bring your own wine.

Tearoom: Soup, toasties, macaroni cheese, date and banana cake (speciality of the house), apricot and nut tea bread, home made scones, broonie (Scot's gingerbread), fresh coffee and a selection of teas.

Opening Times

All year. Tea room open Thursday and Sunday

Prices

From £11.50 B&B

Public Transport Details

To Melvaig (3 miles away)

Facilities

M, F, NR, DA, SD, CH, ES, TC, VR, P, C, V, E

59. "ALLTAN DOMHAIN"

2 Cromasaig
Kinlochewe
By Achnasheen
Ross shire IV22 2PE
Tel: 01445 760 297

Small and friendly B&B run by walking and cycling hosts. Beautifully located at the foot of Beinn Eighe, part of the National Nature Reserve. Superb area for walking, climbing, angling and wildlife eg pine martins, golden eagles. Accesable by public transport. Lock up cycle store and drying facilities.

Contact

Fiona & Clive Hunt

Sample Menu

Several Vegetarian choices. Full breakfast including soysage, home made muesli and oat cakes. Dinner always includes plenty of fresh vegetables and/or salads with Fiona's special dressing. Main course filo pastry filled with leaks, mushrooms, white wine. Spicy red beans with cashew nut rice. cheesy gougere with ratatouille. Deserts: home made ice cream (banana, coffee and sultana, rich chocolate with fresh fruit salad. Apple crumble with sunflower seads and cinamon. Apricot and yoghurt fool with shortbread fans.

Opening Times

All year

Prices

B&B–£16. Dinner £9.00. Lunch £2.50

Public Transport Detail

Train to Achnasheen, then the post bus.

Facilities

M, F, NS, SD, CH, TC, VP, VA, C, A, E

※ 5% discount to readers of this guide

60. OLD SCHOOL BALNACRA

By Strathcarron
Ross-shire
IV54 8YU
Tel: 01520 766224
Fax: 01520 766224

Self catering holiday cottages sleeping 2–5. Wholefood grocery deliveries and vegetarian 'meals on wheels' service.

Sample Menus

Leek brotchan with lemon & parsley.

Brazil nut roast with chestnut stuffing.

Spinach & mushroom lasagne.

Opening Times

All year.

Prices

£100–£300 per week.

Facilities

F, NS, CH, TC, VP, VR, P, C, V, E.

See Map on Page 49

61. CULAG

Carr Brae, Dornie
Kyle of Lochalsh
Ross-shire IV40 8HA
Tel: 01599 555341

Vegetarian/Vegan B & B

Lochalsh & South west Ross is an area of outstanding natural beauty with spectacular mountain and coastal scenery. Great area for walking whether you are a rambler, hillwalker, or mountaineer. The Loch Alsh O.S. Map has 2nd highest number of Munro's & Corbett's (mountains over 3000' & 2500' respectively) second only to that covering Ben Nevis area.

Other attractions include Plockton, Glenelg, Sandaig, Falls of Glonach, exciting wildlife, several craft workshop and sites of historical interest including Eilean Donan Castle, Isle of Skye and Applecross within easy reach.

Contact
Brian Neath

Sample Menus
Breakfast: Fresh fruit salad, savoury pancakes, potato cakes, nut & tomato rissoles, home-made bread, herbal teas, Soya milk.

Dinner: home-made soups & pates, vegetable croustade, parsnip & cashew roast, sponge puddings, and crumbles, apple & tofu whip.

Opening Times
Mid-January to Mid-December

Prices
B&B £15. Dinner £9

Public Transport Detail
Nearest railway station at Kyle of Lochalsh (9 miles). Coach services from Glasgow and Inverness stop in Dornie.

Facilities
J, NS, SD, CH, WHB, TC, VP, VA, C, E

62. CALUM & KATE BULLOCH

Braeintra
By Kyle of Lochalsh
IV53 8UP
Tel.: 01599 577214

Modern detached house with fantastic views and woodland walks starting at the front gate. One double room with futon, one twin, and two single rooms.

Contact
Calum & Kate Bulloch

Sample Menus
Breakfast: Fruit/Yoghurt, local cheeses, oatcakes, bread, pancakes or herb/cheese omelettes, herb tea/tea/real coffee. All cheeses/yoghurts from local West Highland dairy farm. Snacks - soup, salad, cheese toasties.

Prior warning for dinners.

Opening Times
Ring to check

Prices
£15.00 per night. Children under 12 half price. Dinners booked in advance £10.

Public Transport
Train from Inverness

Facilities
VP, CH, TC, V

63. SEAGREEN RESTAURANT & BOOKSHOP

Plockton Road
Kyle of Lochalsh
IV40 8DA
Tel.: 01599 534388

Friendly, spacious, relaxed café/restaurant serving food prepared and cooked on the premises. Blackboard menu and counter service all day, a la carte dinner menu in the evenings. Children very welcome. Easy parking. 'Rough Guide to Scotland', 'Egon Ronay', 'Just a Bite', 'Let's Go', 'Taste of Scotland' etc. recommended, Bookshop stocks mind, body and spirit titles and children's books. Wholefood shop, Photographic and painting exhibitions throughout the season.

Sample Menus

Lunch: Green pea and leek soup with fresh tarragon, cashew nut and tofu dip served with tortilla chips, aubergine red wine and lentil moussaka, organic pasta in parsley and pesto sauce, fresh fruit salad, apple and bramble pie, home baking

Dinner: Aubergine bake with mozzarella cheese and tomato sauce, melon in yoghurt mead and ginger sauce, leek roulade filled with mixed wild mushrooms and crowdie cheese, chestnut and sage roast served with red wine sauce, damson roulade served with crème fraiche, apricot and poppy seed cake served with cashew nut cream, chocolate fudge tart with ewes milk ice cream selection of local cheeses.

Opening Times

Mid March to mid January. Spring and winter – 7 days 10.30am–5pm / Late Spring and summer – 7 days 10am-9pm

Prices

Lunch: (main course) £3.65 - £4.95 Dinner: £6.95 - £12.50. Snacks: £1.35 - £2.45

Facilities

F, NS, DA SD, L,VP,V

64. THE OLD SCHOOLHOUSE LICENSED RESTAURANT

65

Tigh Fasgaidh
Erbusaig
Kyle of Lochalsh
IV40 8BB
Tel.: 01599 534369
Fax: 01599 534369

Former schoolhouse in peaceful location, between Kyle and Plockton. Mellow atmosphere.

Contact

Calum Cumine

Sample Menus

Breakfast: Muesli, fresh fruit, dried fruit salad, sesame coated cheese.

Dinner: veggie-haggis, soup, crudités and goats cheese in a mint yoghurt dressing; Lentil bake in fresh tomato sauce, aubergine curry, Most desserts and cheeses veggie friendly.

Opening Times

April–mid-November 7pm–10.30pm

Prices

B&B £18–£24 per person per night. Meals £11–£14 for 3 courses approx.

Public Transport Details

Train or bus Inverness–Kyle

Post bus from Kyle to Plockton available

Situated 3 miles from Kyle.

Facilities

M, F, SR, NR, DA, DF, CH, WHB, TC, L, P, C

See Map on Page 49

65. LANGDALE HOUSE

Waterloo Breakish
Isle of Skye
IV42 8QE
Tel.: 01471 822 376
Fax: 01471 822 376

Modern double bungalow. Last house on shore road, overlooking Broadford bay and sea down to Wester Ross. Wildlife including seals viewable from lounge. Bedrooms have TV and satellite. Licensed, dinner available.

Contact

Mrs M A.B. MacGregor

Sample Menus

Breakfast: All usual items including muesli, yoghurt, veg-burgers, sausage, decaffeinated coffee, fruit & herb teas - free range eggs, full & varied menu of home cooking changes daily

Dinner: Request for favourites examples home made soups. Dressed avocado, Vegetable curries, leek & potato pie, lentil lasagne, moussaka, home-made desserts, coffee, biscuits and vegetarian cheeses.

Opening Times

March–November inclusive

Prices

B&B all en suite £20 per person. 4-course dinner £15 per person.

Public Transport Details

Local bus from Skye bridge asking off at "Waterloo". Langdale House last property on right of Waterloo which is a single track road round the edge of Broadford bay.

Facilities

M, F, NS, SD, CH, WHB, TC, L, VR, P, C, V

66. SEAGULL RESTAURANT

Breakish
Nr. Broadford
Isle of Skye
Tel. 01471 822001

Great fresh food in relaxing informal atmosphere, where all meals are truly home cooked with natural ingredients only, including local free range eggs, herbs and salad vegetables. At least one vegetarian soup, several snacks/starters and 2-3 main courses to choose from. the bigger the demand for vegetarian food, the more choice we can offer. We also have a selection of minerals and crystals from around the world for sale.

Contact

Vichar or Tamrasi

Sample Menus

Broccoli and stilton bake, Tofu & tomato gratin with grilled vegetables, Oyster-mushrooms in cream and wine.

Opening Times

Daily 5.00pm - 10.00pm

Prices

£6–£8 main course.

Facilities

M, F, DA, DF, SD, L, VR, C

67. QUIRAING LODGE

Staffin
Isle of Skye
IV51 9JS
Tel.: 01470 562 330

A warm and friendly family home specialising in personal caring for our guests. Spectacular shore line position with panoramic views. Seven twin or family bedrooms, sitting room, dining room, library, sanctuary, most with open fires or stoves. Bikes for hire £5 per day, £3 half day.

Contact Name

Kate Money

Sample Menus

Breakfast- homemade wholemeal bread, porridge, home made yoghurt, cooked breakfast, fruit compote. Lunch: homemade soup, bread, cheese and fruit. Dinner:walnut pate, stuffed tomatoes, curried lentil soup, creamed mushroom pasta, aubergine nut crumble, home made ice cream, stuffed courgettes, apple and almond pie, blackcurrent fool.

Opening Times

All year

Prices

From £16.00 B&B.
£8 evening meal Concessions for under 12s. Packed lunch £2.50

Public Transport Details

Plane/train/bus to Inverness or Glasgow, then direct bus service from both to Portree.

Facilities

J, SD, CH, WHB, TC, VP, VR
C, V (on request), E

68. WHITEWAVE ACTIVITIES

19 Linicro
Kilmuir
Isle of Skye
IV51 9YN
Tel.: 01470 542 414

Comfortable accommodation, at relaxed activity centre with disabled access. Our licensed café specialises in home baking, real soups and proper coffee, Evening meals are vegetarian, with seafood options. Based in a renovated croft house we have double and family rooms, great sunsets, music and friendly atmosphere. We can take you kayaking, teach you to windsurf or hire you a mountain bike. Archery, guided walks, and environmental adventures also available, or just do your own thing, active or otherwise! Gaelic spoken.

Opening Times

All year

Prices

From £1.70–£7 (soup to main meal). B&B from £15. F/Board from £29

69. KENSALROAG HOUSE

Dunvegan
Isle of Skye
IV55 8GZ
Tel. 01470 521306

Vegetarian/vegan B & B. Warm welcome in our traditional croft house, 2 minutes walk from seashore. Dunvegan Castle 2 miles. One double/family room, 1 twin/group room, 1 single. H/C in all rooms, tea coffee; breakfast room, lounge with TV

Contact

Jane Trevelyan

Sample Menus

Breakfast: Buffet, Fresh stoned fruit, yoghurt home-made bread & rolls, vegetarian pate, plus cereals, dried fruit & nuts.

Dinner: (by prior arrangement only), Carrot & coriander soup, baked stuffed aubergines, bean & vegetable bake, rhubarb & ginger crumble, blackcurrant ice cream, Organic where available.

Opening Times

April to November

Prices

B& B £14. Dinner £8–£12

Public Transport Details

School bus to and from Portree once a day.

Facilities

J, NS, CH, WHB, TC, VP, VA, C, V, E
P (by arrangement)

70. TABLES HOTEL & RESTAURANT

Dunvegan
Isle of Skye
IV55 8WA
Tel.: 01470 521404

A small "home from home" hotel & restaurant, centrally situated in the village and overlooking Loch Dunvegan and MacLeod's Tables Mountains. Five bedrooms (4 en suite) STB 3 Crowns commended.

Contact

Mrs Jan MacDonald

Sample Menus

Breakfast: All the usuals plus veggie sausages, scrambled tofu, decaffeinated coffee and tisanes.

Lunch: Snacks and light meals, home-made soups and pates, pies, ploughman's.

Dinner: table d'hôte changes daily. eg Brussel sprouts and almond soup, celery and coconut mousse, aubergine filo pastry roll, butter bean and courgette crumble, chocolate and almond charlotte and plum cheesecake.

Opening Times

All year

Prices

Winter from £20 per person per night B&B. Summer from £24 per person per night B&B

Public Transport Details:

Car recommended, School bus from Portree. Bicycles available. Situated at the junction of the AA50 and A863 roads.

Facilities

M, F, NS, NR, DF, SD, CH, WHB, TC, L, VR, C, V

71. BAILLEBOIDEACH

4 Lephin, Glendale
Isle of Skye
IV55 8WJ
Tel.: 01470 511376
Fax: 01470 511376

Warm friendly welcome at modern crofthouse, with coloured Shetland sheep, in lovely glen with view to Outer Hebrides, 1 double and 2 twin rooms, bathroom with shower. Separate toilet. Please book evening meal by midday.

Contact

Janet Kernachan

Sample Menus

Breakfast:Potato scones, free range eggs, herby tomatoes, home-made bread and marmalades.

Packed lunch: Salads, fruit, home-made cake.

Dinner: Cream and chunky soups, pates, Tuscan bean stew, Lebanese lentils, leek & celery pilaff, fruit salads, crumbles, steamed sponges, ice creams, with butterscotch sauce etc.

Opening Times

January–December (closed October)

Prices

£14.50 per person B&B. £8 per person dinner

Public Transport Details

Take B884 from Dunvegan, 7 miles single track road to Glendale Post office Turn left at Post Office and drive 200 metres.

Facilities

M, F, NS, SD, P, C, V, A, E

72. NEVIS VIEW

69

14 Farrow Drive, Corpach
Fort William PH33 7JW
Tel.: 01397 772 447
Fax: 01397 772 800
Mobile: 0589 535036

Nevis View is a family home in a quiet location with good views of the surrounding countrywide. A good base for exploring the local area. All rooms are comfortably furnished, and a warm welcome awaits you! Single/double/family rooms available. Clock/radio and colour TV in all bedrooms Drying facilities. STB listed/commended Welcome Host

Contact

Mrs Barbara Grieve

Sample Menus

Breakfast: Porridge, tomatoes, eggs, mushrooms, yoghurt. Dinner: Coconut & Lentil pate, humus, soups, mango compote, toasted avocado, provencal courgette & tomato gratin, chick peas with spinach (nvig)/ veggie chilli con carne, pasta dishes, salads; hot maple syrup, bananas with ice cream, caramel custard, pancakes, carob pudding.

Opening Times

All year

Prices

Double/twin from £14.00 per person. Single from £18.00. Evening meal £9.00. Children sharing room with adult/s from £7.00 Packed lunches £2.50

Public Transport Details

Take A830 (to Mallaig) from A82, approx 2 miles north of Fort William. Farrow Drive is on the right, exactly 1/10 mile after Corpach Hotel. Nevis View is 2/10 mile from this turning, on the right.

Facilities

M, F, NS, SD (with prior notice), CH, TC, VP, VR, P, C, V, E

73. RHU MHOR GUEST HOUSE

Alma Road
Fort William
Inverness-shire
PH33 6BP
Tel.: 01397 702213

Rhu Mhor has been in my family since 1972 and is set in an acre of steep wild garden above the town. A traditional guest house with interesting things inside and out. Given warning we can cater for almost any diet. (see brochure).

Contact

Ian MacPherson

Sample Menus

Egg, Glamorgan sausage, fried pancake, mushroom, juice home-made marmalade, fresh oven scones, porridge etc. Vegetarian stroganoff home-made soups asparagus and mushroom pasta, clootie dumpling.

Opening Times

April to October

Prices

B&B £17–£17.50. Dinner £10–£10.50

Public Transport Details

Close to railway station and bus stances.

Facilities

M, F, SD, CH, WHB, TC, VP, VR, P, C, V, E

74. CAFÉ BEAG

Fort William
Inverness-shire
PH33 6SY
Tel.: 01397 703601

Our café is a timber building at the foot of Ben Nevis. The food is all home cooked and the atmosphere is relaxed and friendly, you can stay for a meal, a snack, or just a browse round the shop. We hire walking boots, rucksacks and child carriers. Licensed.

Sample Menus

Breakfast: Full Veggie, beans on toast, eggs on toast. Lunch: Omelettes, toasties, salad, veggie soup, veggie burgers. Dinner: garlic bread, pancakes filled with mushroom stroganoff, stuffed aubergines au gratin, bean casserole, vegeatble lasagne.

Opening Times

Mid March–end October 8am–10pm every day.

Prices

Lunch (main course) £3- £5. Dinner (main course) £5-£7.

Public Transport Detail

Three miles up Glen Nevis beside the Youth Hostel.

Facilities

M, F, NS, DA, DF, VP, VR,L, V

Onich
Nr. Fort William
PH33 6SD
Tel. 01855 821529

Spectacular west coast mountain and loch scenery. A friendly welcome, comfortable Victorian house in large interesting garden. Walking, climbing, cycling, skiing (Glencoe & Nevis range) and just relaxing. One twin, 2 double, lounge with log fire, drying room. Shower/bath always available.

Contact

Lisa Glaze

Sample Menus

Breakfast: Fruit juice, fresh grapefruit, porridge, full vegetarian cooked breakfast including potato scone and sausages, free range eggs, fresh baked rolls, cafetiere coffee, herb teas hot chocolate.

Dinner: home-made soup, lasagne, lentil and spinach quiche, winter vegetable crumble, fresh fruit Pavlova, cheese and oatcakes, coffee.

Opening Times

January–November

Prices

B&B £15 per person. Evening meal £10 winter only (must book). Packed Lunch £3.50 (please book day before)

Public Transport Details

Onich lies 8 miles south of Fort William on A82 Glasgow road. Train to Fort William. Buses from Glasgow and Fort William.

Facilities

J, NS, CH, WHB, TC, VP, VR, C, V, E

Glencoe
Nr. Fort William
PA39 4HL
Tel. 01855 811660
Fax 01855 821463

Experience for yourself the energy of the myths and legends which have so power-fully governed the people here for centuries past. Five fabulous indoor attractions. Vegetarian most welcome with a selection of mouth-watering dishes served in the Viking foodship: Norwegian soup, delicious vegetarian moussaka and a selection of tasty salads!

Contact

Graeme Robertson

Opening Times

10–6pm

Prices

Adult £4.95. Child £2.95 . OAP £2.95. Family (2 adults 2 children) £12

Facilities

V, E

So why should you join The Vegetarian Society?

- **Because** we've been working on behalf of vegetarians for nearly 150 years.

- **Because** it's kinder to animals, to people, to the world in which we live.

- **Because** you'll be entitled to discounts at hundreds of restaurants and health food stores throughout the country.

- **Because** you'll receive 4 issues of *The Vegetarian* magazine per year, packed with advice and information from the experts.

- **Because** we receive no government funding and rely on your support to help finance our programme of education and campaigning.

Act Now!

Fill in the coupon, or ring Janet on
0161 928 0793 with your credit card details

Yes I'd like to join The Vegetarian Society and help support its vital work

12 month membership of The Vegetarian Society

❏ Adult £21 ❏ Student/unwaged £16
❏ Family membership £26 ❏ Junior £8

Annual fees include 4 quarterly issues of *The Vegetarian*

For overseas membership please **add** £7 for Europe or £10 for countries outside Europe

I enclose a cheque for £ ....
made payable to *The Vegetarian Society*

Name: ....

Address: ....

....

Postcode: .... Tel: ....

Return to: The Vegetarian Society, Parkdale, Dunham Road, Altrincham, Cheshire WA14 4QG A registered charity

The Western Isles of Lewis, Harris, North and South Uist, Benbecula and Barra are probably better known (at least to me) as The Outer Hebrides, but in fact they are not as far 'outer' as The Orkneys and The Shetlands. There is also a lot more of them than I thought there was (ho-hum)...

Lewis
by Deb Nash

Lewis has a population of about 18,000 spread over a large area. It features a unique Gaelic-speaking culture particular rich in traditional music. Diverse occupations include the famous 'Harris tweed weavers' and seaweed harvesters. The landscape changes dramatically from area to area, north and east Lewis are fairly flat while the south and the west are mountainous. There are huge tracks of moorland and vast, empty, clean beaches. You might see otters, all sorts of sea birds, waders, unusual migrants and garden birds. You must visit the Callanish Stones, a breathtaking stone circle. There are also many other sites of archaeological interest, the Blackhouse museum, a restored blackhouse village, a folk museum and Lewis castle. Stornoway is able to provide most things for most people, there are also local shops and a mobile everything, from grocers to banks. You can reach the island by ferry from Ullapool to Stornoway, or from Uig (Skye) to Tarbert also there are flights from Glasgow or Inverness to Stornoway. Once here, there are buses to all areas and hitch-hiking is easy – most people are willing to give assistance. This is a very religious community, no shops are open on Sunday nor is there any no local transport – even the local swings are chained up! Most hotels are open on a Sunday but some B&Bs will not accept incoming guests.

Harris
with help from Paula Williams

Harris is mountainous, the highest point at Anchisham reaches 799 metres. There are excellent challenges here for walkers, with a rocky east coast contrasting with the fertile west coast which has many splendid beaches; North Harris has some dramatic hills. There are many religious buildings here including St Clement Church which contains the sculptured tomb of Alasdair Crotach Macleod who apparently made this tomb himself some 19 years before he died in 1547. There is now a car-ferry several times a day from and to North Uist and a new bus service should make getting around easier.

North & South Uist, Benbecula, Barra & Vatersay

North Uist has rolling hills and moorland and that oh, so beautiful white sand. It connects to Benbecula at Grimsay bay via a causeway and bridge, and another causeway joins to South Uist. Historic Eriskay lies to the southeast of South Uist and along the west coast are sand dunes coloured by wild orchids and green grassland. Flora MacDonald, famous for helping Bonnie Prince Charlie to escape, was born here. Off the north coast lies Berneray which is now the only populated island in the south, the rest of the islands were cleared of people in the 19th century. A birdwatchers' paradise, the RSPB has a nature reserve on North Uist. Barra & Vattersay form the Southern tip of the Hebridean Island chain. On Barra there are over 1000 species of wild flowers which confirms that 'small is beautiful'. These islands are rich in archaeological sites, and many castles and religious buildings can be seen including Kisimul Castle on Barra.

Although I have given all the place names in English you will see their Gaelic equivalent but most are fairly easy to translate.

Orkney

Orkney is actually a group of seventy islands just six miles north of the Scottish Mainland. Around 120,000 people visit Orkney every year. They come to see villages, forts, burial chambers and standing stones pre-dating the pyramids in Egypt. They come to see the 'Old Man of Hoy', unusual birds, fabulous flowers and miles of sandy beeches. Islands of extreme seasons, it has light for almost 24 hours around the summer solstice.

The Orcadians are proud to tell you that they have time for each other and for you, and that no question, no matter how unusual, will go unanswered.

Every Christmas Day and New Year's Day ,a street football match takes place involving some two hundred players and one ball – the game finishes only when a goal has been scored at the other end of the street or in the sea! Apparently some unenlightened visitors have mistaken this event for a street riot...

There are many mysteries still left in Orkney – like what really happened at Skara Brae, and was the ring of Brodgar a lunar observation platform?

Shetland

Rumour has it that the Romans sailed this far north but declined to stay. Others did stay however, the Vikings, the Norsemen and the Danes all made

Shetland their home and in fact for 600 years Shetland was ruled by Scandinavia, until it was given to Scotland as a dowry! The Vikings may have long since departed but their presence will be felt forever. On the winter solstice, the festival of 'Up Helly Aa' features a procession of a 1000 torch carrying revellers, a squad of Vikings and a Viking longship which is ceremoniously burned.

Only fifteen out of over one hundred Shetland Islands are inhabited and that is good news for the abundance of wildlife that live here. The Isle of Foula, 26 miles west of the mainland, and Fair Isle to the south, offer the adventurer inspiration and isolation. Muckle Flugga has Britain's most northerly port. In winter watch out for the Northern Lights (Aurora Borealis) – although these are supposed to be seen throughout the Highlands and Islands, I have not seen them in the three winters I have been here, indeed they are proving rarer than a sighting of Nessie or a Vegetarian haggis!

DON'T MISS! *Old Man of Hoy, Skara Brae*

Western Isles Tourist Board	**Shetland Tourist Board**	**Orkney Tourist Board**
26 Cromwell Street	Market Cross	6 Broad Street
Stornoway	Lerwick	Kirkwall
Isle of Lewis	HS21 2DD	Shetland ZE1 0LU
Orkney	KW15 1NX	Tel: 01851 703088
Tel: 01595 693434	Tel: 01856 872856	Fax: 01851 705244
Fax: 01595 695807	Fax: 01856 875056	

Health Food Shops

Health Craft
2 Commercial Road, Lerwick   01595 692924

Stornoway Grain & Health Food Store
5 Cromwell Street, Stornoway   01857 702255

Rainbows & Wellies
the taigh na mara cookbook

*First edition hardback, ringbound signed copies are
available from the authors for £16.95 including
post & packing.
Tel. 01854 655282 with credit card details,
or write to Fior Iomhaigh, The Shore, Ardindrean,
Lochbroom, Nr Ullapool IV32 2BR*

77. PAULA WILLIAMS B&B

2 Glen, Leverburgh
An T Ob
Harris
PA83 3TY
Tel: 01859 520 319

Relaxed and comfortable traditional crofthouse. Guests own dining room and sitting-room with open fire and books. One double, 1 family & 1 twin. Good base for touring the islands.

Contact Name

Paula Williams

Sample Menus

Breakfast: Home-made breads, porridge, muesli, yoghurt, fruit, free range eggs.

Evening Meal: Soups – carrot & lovage, fresh tomato, borscht, Stir fries, savoury pasta, mushroom bake, salads, fresh fruit puddings and cakes.

Opening Times

January–December

Prices

B&B £16. Evening meals £10–£12

Public Transport Details

1 mile Leverburgh (An t-ob) ferry 20 miles Tarbert. Several buses daily. Ideal situation for beaches and hillwalking.

Facilities

M, F, NS, NR, SD, CH, TC, VR, P, C, V, E

78. THE WILLOWS

19 Tolsta Chaolais
Isle of Lewis
PA86 9DW
Tel: 01851 621321

Lochside crofthouse in beautiful location, offering 1 twin room with private bath and living rooms. Wonderful walking, bird and wildlife. Three miles Callanish stones. Friendly hosts, no pressure to go out if you don't feel like it!

Vegetarian Society Food & Drink Guild Member

Contact

Deb & David Nash

Sample Menus

Breakfast: Veggie "British" breakfast - vegetarian sausages, beans, mushrooms, egg, tomato, etc. Or fresh fruit, yoghurt etc.

Dinner: Curries, pasta, chilli's etc. Four courses of excellent home cooking.

Opening Times

All year

Prices

B&B £16. Dinner (4 course) £11

Public Transport Details

Ferry:Ullapool–Stornoway or Uig–Tarbert. Bus: Stornoway–Carloway. Ask to be put down at N.W. Autopoint garage. Ring us if doubtful or stuck!

Facilities

J, SR, NR, DA, SD, CH, TC, VP, VA, P (by arrangement), V, E

79. HARBOUR VIEW

Port of Ness
Isle of Lewis
HS2 0XA
Tel.: 01851 810735

Comfortable B&B and tea-room in characterful old boat builder's house situated above picturesque harbour and beautiful beach. One double, 1 twin with WHB, T/C, residents lounge. STB one Crown commended. Candlelit four course dinner for non residents (booking essential) Also craft and gift shop with original paintings and prints of island scenes.

Contact

Kate & Anthony Barber

Sample Menus

Breakfast: Porridge with whisky, muesli, sautéed mushrooms or poached egg with parsley butter on potato cake, omelettes, toast and preserves.

Lunch: Home-made soups, toasted sandwiches, pate jacket potatoes quiche herbal teas home-baking.

Dinner: oven baked peppers, savoury cheese croquettes, stilton & celery flan, red wine & red kidney bean lasagne, mushroom risotto, baked bananas in apricot sauce double lemon pudding, vanilla ice cream with hot apples, honey & spices.

Opening Times

Tearoom March–November Monday–Saturday 11am–5.30pm. B&B all year

Prices

B&B £16– £19. Evening meal £10–£12.50. Packed lunch: £3.50

Facilities

F, NS, NR, SD, CH, WHB, TC, VP, VR, C, V, E

80. WOODWICK HOUSE

Evie, Orkney
KW17 2PQ
Tel: 01856 751330
Fax: 01856 751383

Set in 12 acres of woodland, we are in an ideal situation from which to explore the main ancient sites and RSPB Reserves. Seal watching and music evenings.

Contact Name

Ann Herdman

Sample Menus

Fruit compote, cheese and mushrooms, our own free range eggs. Home made marmalade.

Lunch: home-made soup with fresh soda bread and local cheeses and salads.

Dinner: Carrot roulade with savoury mushroom filling and creamy sauce with a selection of starters an desserts all home-made and using local produce.

Opening Times

All year

Prices

B& B £20–£36 depending on time of year and whether en suite is required.

Public Transport Details

From the A965 turn off to Evie after about 15 mins. turn right. After the sign to Woodwick House turn 1st left and follow road to the end.

Facilities

M, F, NR, DA, DF, SD, CH, WHB, TC, L, VP, VR, P, C, V, E

81. BURRASTOW HOUSE

Walls
Shetland
ZE2 9PB
Tel.: 01595 809 307
Fax : 01595 809 213

Hotel and Restaurant.

Contact Name
Bo Simmons

Sample Menus
Lassi, pancakes, muffins, croissant. Pasta with wild mushrooms and saffron sauce, baba ganoush, humus vegetarian moussaka spinach soufflé tomato and cress roulade, vegetable goulash.

Opening Times
12.30–2.30pm & 7.30pm–9pm

Prices
Lunch a la carte starter £2+ (including salad & veg) main course £7.95 pudding £2 coffee/tea/herbal tea £1.50. Dinner set £28.50. 3 courses & cheese, coffee and truffles.

Public Transport Details
Bus to Walls. Two miles from Walls up hill, turn left on brow hill follow to end of road.

Facilities
M, F, SR, NR, DA, DF, SD, CH, WHB, TC, L (Table), VP, VR, C, V, A, E
P (a great variety)

82. BAYANNE HOUSE

Sellafirth Yell
Shetland
ZE2 9DG
Tel: 01957 744 219
Fax: 01957 744 219
e-mail:
tony.gott@zetnet.co.uk

Eighteenth Century merchant's house on the beach at Basta Voe, Yell. Ideal location for bird and otter watching and within easy reach of R.S.P.B. reserves. We are a croft, growing and producing much of our own food. A guide, tours and local information always available.

Contact Name
Tony & Liz Gott

Sample Menus
Breakfast: Muesli, home-made bread and preserves, fresh free range eggs, home-made goats milk, yoghurt and cheese.

Dinner: wild mushroom risotto, lentil and cheese wedges, vegetable curries, home-made pasta all with organic garden produce.

Opening Times
All year

Prices
Dinner B& B £21

Public Transport Details
Overland bus service to and from Lerwick daily, connecting with a regular inter-island ro-ro ferry service.

Facilities
F, NS, SD, CH, TC, VR, V, E

ISLAND HOPPING?

TOURIST BOARD	ISLAND	DEPART FROM (TO)	TIME
Ayrshire & Aran	Aran	Ardrossan - Brodick	1 hour
	Cumbrae	Largs	10 minutes
Argyll	Ardnamurchan	Tobermory (Mull) - Kilchoan	35 minutes
	Bute	Wemyss Bay - Rothesay	30 minutes
	Coll	Oban (via Mull)	3 hours 5 mins
	Colonsay	Oban	2 hours 15 mins
	Gigha	Tayinloan	20 minutes
	Iona	Fionphort (Mull)	5 minutes
	Islay	Kennacraig - Port Ellen	2 hours 10 mins
	Jura	Islay	5 minutes
	Lismore	Oban	50 minutes
	Mull	Oban - Craignure	40minutes
		Lochaline - Fishnish	15 minutes
	Tiree	Oban (via Mull and Coll)	4 hours 15 mins
Highlands	Canna	Malaig (via Skye,Eigg,Muck,Rum)	5 hours
	Eigg	Malaig (via Skye)	2 hours
	Muck	Malaig (via Skye and Eigg)	2 hours 45 mins
	Raasay	Sconser (Skye)	15mins
	Rum	Malaig (via Skye, Eigg, Muck)	4 hours
	Skye	*Bridge* (Kyle of Lochalsh)	–
		Malaig - Armadale	30 minutes
Western Isles	Barra	Oban - Castlebay	5 hours 15 mins
	Benbecula	*Causeway* (Grimsay)	–
	Berneray	Otternish (N.Uist)	5 minutes
	Harris	Uig (Skye) - Tarbert	1hour 45 mins
	Lewis	Ullapool - Stornoway	2hours 40mins
	Scalpay	Kyles Scalpay	10 minutes
	North Uist	Uig (Skye) - Lochmaddy	1 hour 50mins
	South Uist	Oban (via Barra) - Lochboisdale	7 hours 10mins
Orkney	Orkney	John O'Groats (Foot Passengers only)	45 minutes
		Burwick Aberdeen–Stromness	8 hours
		Lerwick - Stromness	8 hours
		Scrabster - Stromness	1 hour 45 mins
Shetland	Shetland	Stromness - Lerwick (Sunday only)	8 hours
		Aberdeen - Lerwick	14 hours

See Map on Page 49

80

MADE TO LAST LTD.

8 The Crescent
Hyde Park
Leeds
LS7 3JT
Tel: 0113 230 4983

Fed up with damp sweaty feet?

Want some comfortable, waterproof footwear?

We could be the answer to your dreams.

Established in 1984 Made to Last is a small co-operative based in Leeds.

After 10 years of trying, in 1992 we eventually found a none leather material that is waterproof but still allows your feet to breath.

We now make non leather shoes and boots suitable for vegans.

We produce hard wearing casual footwear here at our shop/workshop.

You can choose from over 20 styles and 10 colours, either by coming to see us (to be recommended if you have problem feet) or by Mail Order.

For further information please send a stamped addressed A4 envelope to the above address.

Contact

Liz

PROVAMEL

Vandermoortele (UK) Ltd
Ashley House
86-94 High Street
Hounslow
Middx.
TW13 1NH

Provamel supply a range of soya products, including various types of milk, cream, chocolate and vanilla desserts and a new fresh non-dairy strawberry and peach yoghurt. They boast a range of benefits, such as being lactose free, cholestral free, free of ingredients of animal origin and low in fat.

The **Provamel** range is available from independant health food stores, selected supermarkets and Holland and Barrett.

PROVAMEL

Dairy-free, cholesterol-free,

Yofu

A dairy-free alternative to yoghurt

Yes, it's all true – new Provamel Yofu boasts the many benefits you would normally associate with the P rovamel range of soya products.

With a choice of peach and strawberr y, Provamel Yofu has all the taste of a dair y

VINCEREMOS WINES & SPIRITS LIMITED

261 Upper Town Street
Bramley
Leeds
LS13 3JT
Tel : 0113 257 7545
Fax: 0113 257 6906

We are the UK's longest established importers and wholesalers of independantly certified and award winning Organic and Vegetarian Society approved wines.

We have a range of well over a hundred Organic and Vegetarian wines, beers, ciders and juices . We offer a friendly service and rapid delivery to lowlands, highlands and islands. Trade credit accounts are welcome and we accept Visa, Delta, Switch, Mastercard and cheques for private sales.

Contact

Jem Gardener

We supply Trade and Mail Order customers and offer a special **5% first order discount** *to 'Scotland the Green' readers.*

YOUR BODY LIMITED

Ref STG97/98
Units 52-54
Milmead Ind. Estate
Mill Mead Road
London
N17 9QU
Tel: 0181 808 2662/3
Fax: 0181 801 8498

Mail Order Company

Your Body is a British company who develop and manufacture high quality, cruelty-free and animal-free beauty products in England. None of their finished products are tested on animals, and the company has a fixed cut-off date of 1984 in respect of animal tested ingredients.

Competitively priced, products are based on vegetable, herb, plant and fruit extracts, and aromatic essential oils, exclude lanolin and all animal-derived ingredients. Suitable for vegetarians, vegans and sensitive skin, **Your Body's** extensive range of head to toe beauty products are available by post.

Contact

Jill Baker

Ring now for **FREE** *catalogue quoting REF.STG 97/98*

See Map on Page 49

WHOLE EARTH

269 Portobello Road
London
W11 1LR
Tel: 0171 229 7545
Fax: 0171 221 6416

Cruelty Free shopping – food

Whole Earth began when we opened a macrobiotic restaurant in London frequented by people like The Rolling Stones and The Beatles in the 60s. We are now more famous for our range of food products with an emphasis on high fibre, low sugar, low fat, unrefined, wholesome and organic ingredients. We have never wavered from our commitment to quality and an organic way of living. Award winners for "Best Range of Organic Foods".

Contact

Barbara Coles

The Products

Nut butters, pure fruit spreads, organic baked beans, sauces and ketchups, dressings and relishes, syrups, Wake Cup (coffee alternative), hummus, rice, organic cornflakes and other quality products. Available from all good health food shops

DOLMA VEGAN PERFUMES

19 Royce Avenue
Hucknall
Nottingham
NG15 6FU

History & Ethics

Established in 1982 by a practicing Vegan and qualified chemist to supply perfumes which could be used with confidence by Vegetarians and Vegans. All products are free from animal derived and animal tested substances and are carefully blended from safe, long established Vegan ingredients. 1976 fixed cut-off date.

Products

An exclusive range of high quality original perfumes, aromatic shampoos for the body, hair face and feet, moisturisers, cleansers toners, facial scrubs and masks, hand cream, body lotion, shaving fluid, aftershave (balm & cologne), aromatherapy, facial & massage oils, talcs, soaps and essential oils etc.

(send s.a.e. for free brochure)

PHOENIX COMMUNITY STORES

FOR LOVERS OF GOOD FOOD
NATURAL ◊ ORGANIC ◊ GOURMET

VEGETARIAN

SOUPS, SOYA PRODUCTS, TOFU, TEMPEH, TAMARI, GELATINE, STOCKCUBES, MEAL MIXES, BREAKFAST CEREALS, SPREADS, NUT BUTTERS, GRAINS, CEREALS, NUTS, SEEDS, BEANS, HERBS & SPICES, FLOURS, HONEY, JAMS, CHINESE, THAI, MEXICAN, INDIAN, JAPANESE, PASTA, SAUCES, BISCUITS, CRISPBREADS, OILS, DRESSINGS, OLIVES, CHEESE, FROZEN MEALS, ICECREAM, SOYCREAM, CONDIMENTS, HERB TEAS, COFFEE, FRUIT & VEG, DRIED FRUIT, CORN CHIPS, CAKES, CRISPS, JUICES, CONFECTIONERY ETC.

& ORGANIC

CHEESE, FRUIT, VEGETABLES, BUTTER, MILK, CHOCOLATE, NUTS, SEEDS, GRAINS, BEANS, CEREALS, TEA, COFFEE, BISCUITS, BEER, WINE, JUICE, CRISPBREAD, OATCAKES, CAKES, CORNCHIPS, PASTA, SPICES, SOY PRODUCTS, SOUPS, DRIED FRUIT, BREAKFAST CEREALS, SEASONINGS, BREAD, YOGURT ETC.

& MORE

COOKBOOKS, ORGANIC CLOTHING, ECOLOGICAL CLEANING PRODUCTS, FULL RANGE APOTHECARY, GIFTS, CRAFTS, NEW AGE BOOKS, MUSIC.

WHERE ELSE?

RETAILERS OF QUALITY AND INSPIRATIONAL PRODUCTS
PHOENIX ◊ THE PARK, FINDHORN BAY, MORAY TEL: (01309) 690110
EPICURUS ◊ 9, LEOPOLD ST, NAIRN TEL: (01667) 452874

Animal Aid
Against All Animal Cruelty

Education and campaigns: factory farming, animal experiments, fur trade, pet trade, zoos and circuses.

Information and advice: vegetarianism, living without cruelty, humane research.

If you would like to find out more about the work we do and how you can become involved in helping to fight animal cruelty, please contact us at the address below.

For an information pack and membership details, please send sae to:

strictly peaceful

campaigning

Animal Aid
THE OLD CHAPEL, BRADFORD STREET
TONBRIDGE, KENT TN9 1AW
Tel: (01732) 364546   **Fax: (01732) 366533**

30 MILLION VARIETIES STILL AVAILABLE...

One Scottish organisation campaigns on a wider range of environmental issues than any other, from protecting forests to setting sustainability targets. We depend on people like you to make these campaigns work. Join us and together we can make a difference.

CONTACT: FoE Scotland, 72 Newhaven Rd, Edinburgh, EH6 5QG, or ring 0131 554 9977.

Join

FRIENDS OF THE EARTH SCOTLAND

Dew of BEN NEVIS

Proprietors
BEN NEVIS DISTILLERY (FORT WILLIAM) LIMITED
LOCHY BRIDGE, FORT WILLIAM PH33 6TJ

70cl   Produce of Scotland   40% vol

ACTIVELY PROTECTING ENDANGERED SPECIES — TUSK FORCE

The Tusk Force Scottish Highland Conservation Project

Time is running out for many of Britain's indigenous wildlife. Highland species including the Scottish wildcat and red squirrel, and riverside mammals such as the otter, face a variety of threats from pollution to habitat destruction. If something is not done now to protect our native wildlife the damage will be irreparable.

Tusk Force, a registered endangered species charity, have produced a limited edition series of fine blended Scotch Whisky. The Dew of Ben Nevis has been produced at the Ben Nevis Distillery, in the shadow of the magnificent Ben Nevis mountains, since 1825. With their kind co-operation, and the help of Netherton Promotions, Tusk Force have been able to produce this limited edition series, all profits from which will go towards the protection of endangered Scottish wildlife.

There are four label designs to collect, each of which have been reproduced from original paintings by renowned artist Paul Apps. Individual bottles retail at £19.95, (+ p&p) but we are willing to negotiate a price for bulk buying or trade purchases. If you would like further information, or would like to place an order, please call

Leah McVeigh on 0181-870-4122, or fill in the attached form and return to:

Tusk Force,
FREEPOST 4 Spencer Court,
140-142 Wandsworth High Street,
London SW18 4YY

(Allow 28 days for delivery).

Title: _____ Name: _____   Surname: _____

Address: _____

_____   Post Code: _____

Day Time Telephone: _____   (Vital in case of enquiries)

Total Amount: £ _____   Number of Bottles Ordered: _____

Please indicate which label design/s you would like to receive, by putting the number of bottles required in the relevant box.

☐ Squirrel   ☐ Otter

☐ Cappercaillie   ☐ Eagle

CREDIT CARD ORDERS   Type of Card: Visa   Mastercard/Access   (Delete as applicable)

Card Number: _____   Expires: ___ / ___

The cost of postage and packing, per bottle and carton, is £4.00

CHEQUES/POSTAL ORDERS   If paying by cheque or postal order, please make cheques payable to Tusk Force Ltd.

ACTIVELY PROTECTING ENDANGERED SPECIES — TUSK FORCE

Seagreen

Restaurant
& Bookshop

*Specializing in local seafood
and wholefood dishes*

All food cooked on the premises
All day licensed café • Garden
Wholefood shop • Outside Terrace
Exhibition space • Traditional music
Local interest Literature

Plockton Road, Kyle of Lochalsh
Wester Ross IV40 8DA
Tel 01599 534388

Rua Reidh Lighthouse

Guide walks and Activity Holidays
Melvaig–Gairloch Tel/fax 01445 771263

WhitewaveACTIVITIES

Café & Accommodation

Kayaking•Widsurfing• GuidedWalks

No.19 Linicro, Kilmuir, Isle of Skye
IV51 9YN
Tel. 0147 0542 414

Welcome to
CAFÉ HELIOS
In the Universal Hall

at the Findhorn Foundation Community

surrounded by beautiful gardens and a waterfall

Changing monthly art exhibitions

serving Italian and American coffee, French cakes and pastries,

cold drinks, snacks and freshly prepared lunches.

Opening times: Monday 12.30 – 5pm
Tuesday – Saturday 10 – 5pm & Sunday 12 – 5pm

Animal testing.

Unreliable.

Unethical.

Unnecessary.

NATIONAL **ANTI-VIVISECTION** SOCIETY

Every year millions of animals in laboratories all over the world are burnt, blinded, scalded, crushed, frozen and poisoned to death .... all for experiments that can never be trusted. The National Anti-Vivisection Society (NAVS) works to end these futile and cruel experiments. We lobby Parliament, produce technical reports and fund non-animal medical research.

One of the myths about animal experiments is that they are 'a necessary evil' - that there is no other choice for safety-testing, or for medical progress. These examples of medical progress without animals destroy such a myth -

Drugs - beta blockers for blood pressure; digitalis for heart failure; morphine as a pain killer; nitrite drugs for angina; quinine for malaria; active part of aspirin.

Surgery - removal of appendix, bladder stones, cataracts, removal of the ovaries for tumours, repair of heart aneurysm, and other techniques.

The study of people, their lifestyle and environment, showed the link between **smoking and cancer**, and **causes of heart disease**.

Animal tests give misleading results: There are differences in the way different species respond to the same product

Penicillin - a useful antibiotic for people, but it kills guinea pigs.

Cancer drug - 6-azauridine can be used in humans for long periods, but small doses can kill dogs in a few days.

Tamoxifen - designed as a contraceptive - it is in rats, but in women is has the opposite effect. Used in treatment of breast cancer, despite having caused cancer in rat studies.

If you want to see an end to animal experiments - join the NAVS today.

National Anti-Vivisection Society,
261 Goldhawk Road, London, W12 9PE.
Tel. 0181 846 9777

highland wholefoods

WHOLESALE CASH & CARRY & DISTRIBUTION THROUGHOUT THE HIGHLANDS & ISLANDS

Visit our Cash & Carry & Choose from over 4000 lines

VEGETARIAN•VEGAN•ORGANIC
DELI•DRINKS•HERBS&SPICES
CHILLED•ORG. FRUIT & VEG
ENVIRONMENTALLY AWARE PRODUCTS

PHONE FOR A PRICE LIST TODAY

Unit 6B
13 Harbour Road
INVERNESS IV1 1SY

Tel: 01463 712393
Fax: 01463 715586

Six Mary's Place
Raeburn Place, Stockbridge
Edinburgh

Six Mary's Place Guest House

"A peaceful haven in the heart of the city"

Beautifully restored Georgian townhouse with STB Two Crown Commended status, specialising in Vegetarian cuisine and offering a pleasant smoke-free environment.

Delightful conservatory and restful gardens.

Contact Elaine Gale, Six Mary's Place, Edinburgh EH4 1JH

Tel. 0131 332 8965

http://ourworld.compuserve.com/
homepages_ECT_Social_Firms/smp1.htm

LANCRIGG
VEGETARIAN COUNTRY HOUSE HOTEL

Vegetarian Country House Hotel & Restaurant

Easedale, Grasmere, Cumbria LA22 9QN

Perfect peace and quiet ½ mile from Grasmere village in the heart of the English Lake District.

Delicious wholefood vegetarian cuisine. Licensed.

Luxury four-posters & whirlpool suites.

Robert & Janet Whittington

Tel. 015394 35317 • Fax. 015394 38058

Findhorn Press

Books of Inspiration and Hope

The Press Building, The Park, Findhorn, Forres IV36 0TZ
Tel. 01309 690582 • Fax. 01309 690036
email: thierry@findhorn.org

Call for our latest catalogue or consult our web pages on

http://www.gaia.org/findhornpress/

Confused by green claims?
Want to know where to buy an
environmentally friendly fridge?
What's the alternative to toxic
treatments in the home?

WENDi is part of The Women's Environmental Network Trust a registered charity no.1010397

Women's Environmental Network Directory of Information

WENDI

0171 704 6800

For Information on the
environmental, ethical and health effects of
consumer products- call WENDI-
open Mon- Fri 11 am - 2pm and 3pm -6pm

EDINBURGH

Edinburgh Central, near Playhouse, B&B in Georgian flat
Vegan/vegetarian. Good vegetarian restaurants nearby
Tel. 0131 557 4752 (and answerphone)

Beauty Through Herbs

Leading natural beauty care into the 21st century

1 Sir John's Square, Thurso, Caithness KW14 7AN
Tel. 01847 895558

Port-Na-Con Guesthouse

"A Reputation for Good Food"
Loch Eriboll, Sutherland. Tel. 01771 571367

GLEN FESHIE HOSTEL

Kincraig, Inverness-shire PH21 1NN
Telephone: 01540 651323

Samadhan

Located on the beautiful Scoraig Peninsula, by the side of little Loch Broom, Samadhan offers a uniquely tranquil setting in which to recharge flagging batteries. Surrounded by an abundance of wildlife (eagles, deer, seals, otters, porpoises and dolphins) in this tastefully renovated crofter's cottage with large meditation room, 2½ acres of woodland and organic garden, we cater vegetarian and have a friendly, relaxed attitude. We are open all year round for your workshops, retreats and relaxation.

For further information contact John Sangster at:
Samadhan, Scoraig Peninsula, Dundonnell by Garve,
Wester Ross IV23 2RE • Tel. 01854 633260

Save animals from the carving knife...

join *Viva!*

Viva! is a veggie and vegan charity that fights against cruelty. Contact us today and be a friend of the animals.

Why *Viva!*

Every year in Britain, more than 700 million animals face the barbarity of slaughter – many have their throats slit while they are fully conscious. Most spend their short, brutal lives in misery and pain.

Every year, the earth staggers closer to environmental disaster. Whether polluted water or torched rainforests; global warming or spreading deserts – meat eating is at the heart of the problem. Also, oceans are dying from the constant rape of commercial fishing.

About *Viva!*

Viva! produces loads of free info on being vegetarian or vegan – and campaigns on issues such as factory farming, BSE, slaughter, saving the environment, health and banning live exports. And we can help you change your diet with *Viva! Guides*, all written by experts in their field. We also sell a huge range of veggie books and an eco-tastic range of animal-savin' T-shirts, pens, mugs, stickers, purses, wines, choccies...

And never let it be said that we don't do our supporters proud! When you join you get groovy earth-savin', animal-liberatin', world-warrior stickers, posters and leaflets. Plus, you'll receive either the fab teen mini-mag, *Vivactive!* or *Viva!LIFE* if you are 18 or over.

For FREE info on our latest campaigns, merchandise and details on how to join, send your name, address (and age if under 18) to:

Viva! (Dept. SG), PO Box 212, Crewe, Cheshire CW1 4SD
Or call on 01270 522500 NOW!!

Registered Charity No. 1037486

CUT OUT AND KEEP EMERGENCY MIDGE REPELLANT PAGE

When the scourge of the North is at it's most ravenous in July/August nothing is 100% effective. All you can hope to achieve is to reduce the little blighters enjoyment a little. This special page may be found to help in moments of dire emergency .

Please read following instructions carefully and construct under adult supervision.

1. Using a pair of ordinary household scissors cut along the dotted line
2. Stick page onto a packet of cereal using one of the domestic glues recommended in the Vegan Society's 'Animal Free Shopper'.
3. Cut around the page taking care not to get cereal all over the floor in the process.
4. Your emergency midge repellant page is now ready for use.It now has the following revolutionary anti Highland Midge properties scientifically tested by an Open University student on the shores of Loch Broom

<u>Sight</u>

Bitus
Touristus
Maximus
(million times actual size)

Million times life size artists impression of a psychopathic rogue mad male midge scares pregnant female midges witless.In laboratory tests at least 13.5% of all midges flew in opposite direction.

<u>Touch:</u> Feels just like recyclable paper glued onto an everyday cereal packet confusing the midge leaving it unlikely to suspect the item's midge repellent properties.

<u>Taste:</u> Doesn't taste remotely like the blood of a stressed out rat-race refugee

<u>Smell :</u> This varies greatly depending on the brand of glue used. for added protection dab on some citronella, lavender, or bog myrtle essential oil.

<u>Sound :</u> As a last resort take the page in both hands and wobble board back and forth in a 'Rolf Harris' fashion to the beat of 'Stairway to Heaven' which to be really repulsive to the sonic system of the midge should be sung in an Australian accent "Thairs a laydee whooos shore all thit glittears is gould endt shis by ink eh stare way to heffen wop wop wop wop and it maykes me wondur yeah yeah yeah yeah."

Name _____

Address _____

_____

_____

_____

1. Would you like to receive the next edition of this guide postfree?
   (due to be published in early 1999)

   ☐ yes   ☐ no

2. Where did you purchase this guide?

   _____

3. Did you like the guide? Any improvements you would like to suggest ?

   _____

   _____

4. Which places did you stay in?

   _____

   _____

5. Any you particularly liked and why?

   _____

   _____

6. Or didn't like?

   _____

   _____

7. Any places you can recommend which are not in the current edition of this guide?

   _____

   _____

8. Anything else you would like to tell me

   _____

   _____

   _____

Please return to: Jackie Redding, Fior Iomhaigh, Taigh Na Mara, Freepost IV1229,
An Cladach, Loch Broom Nr Ullapool, Scottish Highlands, IV23 2BR.

IF THE BEEF DOESN'T KILL YOU, I WILL.

Meat may look harmless. It may taste good. But it can kill you. Consider this:

- Some experts speculate that chickens or pigs may have transmitted CJD to humans.

- 54% of frozen and 42% of chilled broiler chickens are infected with salmonella, campylobacter and other potentially deadly bacteria.

- Chicken contains as much Cholesterol as beef and is found ONLY in animal products.

- Eating any meat promotes heart disease, cancer, stroke, obesity and high blood pressure.

- Women who eat eggs daily nearly triple their risk of breast cancer.

The ONLY way to ensure that meat won't kill you is to throw it away.

Call us for FREE vegetarian recipes.
They will blow your mind, not destroy your body.

PeTA PEOPLE FOR THE ETHICAL TREATMENT OF ANIMALS
PO BOX 3169, LONDON NW1 2JF   **0171-388 4922**

A — Z LISTING

A

Abb Cottage 51
Abbey Cottage 17
Achins Coffee Shop 58
Alltan Domhain" 63
An Tairbeart Heritage Centre 35
Archaeolink 39
Argyll Hotel 36
Avingormak Guest House 47

B

Baillieboideach 69
Balgedie Toll Tavern 30
Bayanne House 78
Bruarh Mhor 35
Burrastow House 78
Bute House Hotel 34

C

Café Beag 70
Café Helios 42
Calum & Kate Bulloch 64
Castle of Park 40
Ceilidh Place 59
Chestnut House 14
Choraidh Croft 56
Coffee Shop 57
Craigellachie House 46
Creag-na-Ma 55
Cuildoraig House 71
Culag 64
Culloden Pottery Restaurant 50

D

David Murray 23
Dolma Vegan Perfumes 82

E

Earthward 18

F

Fir Brae Croft House 55

G

Glen Feshie Hostel 47
Glenrannock House 30

Gordon Arms Hotel 39
Grey Gables 18

H

Harbour View 77
Health Works 41
Heloise Shewan 42
Hendersons Salad Table 23
Highland Wholefoods 52
Hydroponicum 58

I

Invercassley Cottage 54
Inverdeen House B&B 38
Iona Cottage 36
Isle of Arran Distilleries 26

J

Janet Anderson 25

K

Kensalroag House 68

L

Ladysmith Guest House 60
Lancrigg Vegetarian Country House 14
Langdale House 66

M

Made to Last Ltd. 80
Mansefield House Hotel 53
Minto House 41
Mountain Restaurant & Lodge 61
Mystery World 71

N

Neptune Guest House 40
Nevis View 69

O

Old Drummond House 51
Old School Balnacra 63
Old School House 65

P

Paula Williams B&B 76
Port-na-Con House 56

Prospect Bank House 24
Provamel 80

Q

Quiraing Lodge 67

R

Rhu Mhor Guest House 70
River Café & Restaurant 52
Rossan 17
Rua Reidh Lighthouse Hotel 62

S

Sail Gairloch 62
Samadhan 61
Seagreen Restaurant 65
Seagull Restaurant 66
Shalimar 50
Six Mary's Place 24
Solus-na-Mar 57
Sonnehalde Guest House 46
Station House 54
Station Tearoom and Craftshop 53
Sunflower Coffee Shop 29

T

Tables Hotel & Restaurant 68
Taigh-na-Mara 60

U

Ubiquitous Chip 25

V

Vinceremos Wines & Spirits Ltd. 81

W

Whitewave Activities 67
Whole Earth 82
Willows (The) 76
Woodwick House 77

Y

Your Body Ltd. 81

Copyright © Jackie Redding 1996

First published 1996

ISBN 1 899171 41 X

Every effort has been made ensure that the information in this book is accurate and up-to-date. However the publishers accept no responsibility for errors, omissions, subsequent alterations or changes.

All rights reserved. The contents of this book may not be reproduced in any form, except for short extracts for quotation or review, without the written permission of the publisher.

British Library Cataloguing-in-Publication Data. A catalogue record for this book is available from the British Library.

Cover illustration by David Gregson. Book layout by Findhorn Press. Background photograph on cover Images©1996 PhotoDisk, Inc. Printed and bound by Interprint Ltd., Malta. Published by Findhorn Press, Scotland.